When Life Takes What Matters

No Rain, No Gain

Discovery House Publishers

Books, music, and videos that feed the soul with the Word of God

Box 3566 Grand Rapids, MI 49501

When Life Takes What Matters

*Devotions to Comfort You
Through Crisis & Change*

No Rain,
No Gain

*Devotions to Guide You
Through the Storms of Life*

Susan Lenzkes

Discovery House Publishers is affiliated with RBC Ministries, Grand Rapids, Michigan 49512.

Discovery House books are distributed to the trade exclusively by Barbour Publishing, Inc., Uhrichsville, Ohio 44683.

Library of Congress Cataloging-in-Publication Data

Lenzkes, Susan L.
    When life takes what matters / Susan Lenzkes.
        p.   cm.
    ISBN 1-57293-057-8
    1. Consolation—Prayer–books and devotions—English.
  2. Suffering—Religious aspects—Christianity. I. Title.
BV4909.L46 1993
248.8'6—dc20   92-31268
                                         CIP

Printed in the United States of America

99 01 03 02 00

CHG

1 3 5 7 9 10 8 6 4 2

When Life Takes What Matters

Devotions to Comfort You
Through Crisis & Change

Lovingly dedicated to my

Dad and Mom
Stacy and Wilda Finefrock

Husband of 32 years
Herb Lenzkes

Mother-in-law
Emma Bare

who now stand in the presence of God
and are probably right now
praying with Christ as He intercedes for us.

Life took a lot of what mattered to me when cancer took first my Mom, then my Dad, and seven months later my husband, Herb. Then strokes took my Mom-in-law. When you lose so much that's precious, you find the rain that is falling in your life is more from your eyes than from the skies.

You also find that you're dealing with these losses in addition to everything else life continues to toss your way. And you don't particularly want to hear any sermons about "growth potential" through it all. You need *comfort*. I know.

So when a person facing some great loss or struggle (such as you face right now) asks which of my books I recommend, I usually suggest *When Life Takes What Matters* because of the understanding and comfort it offers.

But then I inevitably feel a tinge of regret that I didn't suggest *No Rain, No Gain* for the hope it brings to our hurt. And I know how desperately we need that hope, because this fallen world is loaded with dead-end loss and pain.

I thank the dear people at Discovery House Publishers that in the combined pages of these books I can now share both with you. Go ahead and lavish all the comfort and hope you find here on your aching heart. You'll come back and find God always ready with a fresh supply for your next need.

Dear Hurting One

"My mouth would encourage you; comfort from my lips would bring you relief."
—Job 16:5

The measure of loss you are experiencing is
beyond my emotional comprehension.
Yet I ache with you and
long to lift your load,
even while knowing that you alone must carry
one grief at a time to
the God of all comfort.
How I pray that He will lead you daily
to the storehouse of His
grace, compassion, and healing.
And on that day when I need
help through grief's dark night,
I pray that God will grant me
the tender gift of you.

Praise be to the God and Father of our Lord Jesus Christ, the Father of compassion and the God of all comfort, who comforts us in all our troubles, so that we can comfort those in any trouble with the comfort we ourselves have received from God. For just as the sufferings of Christ flow over into our lives, so also through Christ our comfort overflows.

—2 Corinthians 1:3–5

The Truth about Loss

> "In this world you will have trouble. But take heart! I have overcome the world."
> —Jesus (John 16:33)

We *don't like it,* but we know that it's true: trouble is a natural part of living in this fallen world. The lessons come early and stay late.

As babies, we are wet and no one seems to notice. We cry and Mom doesn't rush to pick us up. Then one day we're expected to give up our warm bottle or breast for a cold hard cup. Our favorite blanket disappears in the wash. The stuffing comes out of our teddy bear. "No!" seems to be the answer for everything we want to touch or taste. Daddy keeps walking out the door, and Mommy spends too much time with that bawling little intruder. And these are the normal losses. There are worse.

As children, we find the excitement of going to school is tempered by having to leave the security of home. We learn that "F" stands for failure, not fun. We lose a friend to someone who's prettier or smarter. We are the last one picked for the team. We finally start liking the teacher, then we're promoted to the next grade. And these are the normal losses. There are worse.

As teenagers, we find that our bodies and emotions are a foreign land with ever-changing boundaries. We feel okay about ourselves only if we lose our identity to fads and fashion. A broken romance shreds our heart. Our parents don't understand us. We've lost childhood and can't find adulthood. And these are the normal losses. There are worse.

As adults, instead of celebrating the freedom we expected, we find ourselves tied to a job, a family, and a schedule. Babies cry and throw up. Kids argue and whine. Teens announce their superiority. Our grand dream for how life should be whimpers and slides sideways. People change, disappoint, fail, and leave us. Society is a mess. Gray hairs emerge. We lose our ability to lose weight. The children grow up and move out. Wrinkles and arthritis move in. We can't remember where we put our glasses. And these are the normal losses. There are worse.

We cope with these everyday losses fairly well. We adjust our attitude or change our perspective, method, or approach. Some losses we consciously grieve. Others we hardly notice because they occur so slowly. Occasionally we discover within life's process of loss and change the potential for growth, compassion, or a larger view. Sometimes we settle for simple survival. But we keep moving ahead with creative persistence. This is, after all, life. And these are life's normal losses. There are worse.

Internal losses are worse. These are the deprivations and abuses that seem to be a normal part of life, but are not. They rob us of love, trust, self-esteem, confidence, and a sense of worthiness and leave us feeling inadequate, inferior, unlovable. We bleed internally.

And what about life's land-mine losses? These are the explosions we never expected, didn't deserve, and couldn't prevent. They rip our world apart, leaving gaping holes where something, or someone, important used to be. They strike at our foundation and leave us lonely, lost, frightened, angry, insecure, and needy.

How do we deal with *these*, life's worst kind of losses?

If we're wise, we treat them with tenderness, patience, and God's help. We are hurting because we have serious wounds that need healing. And healing takes time. It also takes cooperation with God.

He whose hand formed us knows how to put us back together when life's losses have left us in pieces. Whether we are being pruned, tested, or have simply been caught in the rain that "falls on the just and the unjust," He will bring us through. He is the great Healer. He is unequaled at creating something from nothing. He even knows how to bring life from death. So certainly we can trust Him with our pain, our loss, our brokenness, our very lives.

Perhaps too it will help to realize that we are more practiced in dealing with loss than we know. After all, we've made it this far.

"For I know the plans I have for you," declares the LORD, "plans to prosper you and not to harm you, plans to give you hope and a future."
—Jeremiah 29:11

Record my lament; list my tears on your scroll—are they not in your record?   —Psalm 56:8

"I have heard your prayer and seen your tears; I will heal you."
—2 Kings 20:5

"I am with you and will save you," declares the LORD. "I will restore you to health and heal your wounds."
—Jeremiah 30:11, 17

The Shape of a Question

> God is more concerned about what is happening *in* me than what is happening *to* me.
>
> —Gordon R. Bear

Life wasn't going the way it was supposed to go. Its continuing trouble and heartache were weighing me down with a leaden "why"-shaped question mark that wound itself around my neck. I took the question to my husband, hoping for an answer. He had none.

Of all my wise and wonderful friends, at least three can be counted on for an insightful opinion on nearly any subject, especially if asked. I asked. Not only did they have no opinion, they had no clues. One friend, the one I was positive would have some sort of an answer whether I liked it or not, said, "I'm as puzzled as you are about this."

Another friend listened as my long string of recent losses shaped itself into the giant question mark. Then she heard me stab the point at its end as I cried out, "What is God trying to tell me with all of this?"

"I'm afraid I have no answer for that," she said gently, "but may I pray for you?" And she did, right there on the phone.

It wasn't long after her loving prayer that I began to understand a rule about questioning God. If I'm asking and not seeming to get an answer, perhaps I'm asking the wrong question. Maybe it needs to be rephrased—or redirected.

My question needed both. And when I gave it some room to maneuver, I found it deliberately curving back at me and rephrasing itself. It no longer asked, What is God trying to tell me? Instead it asked, What have I been telling God by my reaction? Perhaps I've been telling Him that I don't trust Him. That I don't believe He's in control. That He's not the giver of good gifts. Or that He doesn't really have my best interest at heart.

And then the question mark relaxed its crooked posture and reformed itself into a very straight, very confident, very pointed exclamation mark. My own attitude was the problem!

It was time to put away the childish measuring stick that uses circumstances to measure the love and charac-

ter of God. It was time to reaffirm the truth that God is good, holy, just, sovereign, wise, and that He is Love—pure and beautiful. So I deliberately stopped asking "why" and "what" and began to ask "how."

"How, Lord, are You going to bring good for me and glory for You out of all of this?"

I'm so glad that God's results are not limited by His raw materials! I am waiting and watching. I love the way He works—first *in* me, then *around* me.

Therefore, my dear friends . . . continue to work out your salvation with fear and trembling, for it is God who works in you to will and to act according to his good purpose.

—Philippians 2:12–13

Dear friends, don't be bewildered or surprised when you go through the fiery trials ahead, for this is no strange, unusual thing that is going to happen to you. Instead, be really glad—because these trials will make you partners with Christ in his suffering, and afterwards you will have the wonderful joy of sharing his glory in that coming day when it will be displayed. . . .

So if you are suffering according to God's will, keep on doing what is right and trust yourself to the God who made you, for he will never fail you.

—1 Peter 4:12–13, 19 LB

Facing
the Pain

———— ⚜ ————

"If I say, 'I will forget my complaint, I will change
my expression, and smile,' I still dread all my sufferings."
—Job 9:27–28

I pushed against the
pain
the terrible sadness
the dreaded despair.
I said,
"This is no way to live.
Life is too short.
To be victorious
I will rise above the pain."
But loss said,
"This is no way to live.
Life is too short
to pretend it doesn't hurt.

*To be victorious,
go through the pain
toward the promise."*

Humble yourselves, therefore, under God's mighty hand, that he may lift you up in due time. Cast all your anxiety on him because he cares for you.

Be self-controlled and alert. Your enemy the devil prowls around like a roaring lion looking for someone to devour. Resist him, standing firm in the faith, because you know that your brothers throughout the world are undergoing the same kind of sufferings.

And the God of all grace, who called you to his eternal glory in Christ, after you have suffered a little while, will himself restore you and make you strong, firm and steadfast. To him be the power for ever and ever. Amen.

—1 Peter 5:6–11

This Moment

We have this moment
to hold in our hands,

And to touch as it slips
through our fingers like sand;

Yesterday's gone,
and tomorrow may never come,

But we have this moment today.

This will be my first Mother's Day without my mother. Last year she was here, though just barely. It was the last Sunday of her life.

We spent the day with her in the oncology ward. Cancer had taken almost everything it could rob from her body. Yet her spirit rose above the tubes and needles, above the gaunt misery, determined to be present with her husband, children, and grandchildren—determined to give back more love than her frail body could possibly hold.

"That dress!" she rallied to say as I walked into the room. "It's the one from the catalog, the one *I* said you should order, isn't it?"

"You picked it, Mom!" I said, twirling its lavender skirt and smiling at her smiling at me. How could her eyes still have that I-love-life, I-love-pretty-things, I-love-you twinkle?

"I knew it would look great on you," she sighed, her eyes closing briefly against the heaviness of the effort to be there.

And then she received the flowers, the gifts, the words, the love, *the moment.* We knew it was all we could give her. Why hadn't we always known it?

The moment. And whatever we have in our hand and heart. That's all.

It's easy to forget that truth on ordinary days, when death is just as imminent but not so frighteningly obvious. If only we could learn to rise above the circumstances of our moments, however difficult they might be, and share heart-to-heart. Life would surely feel better, indeed, *be* better. After all, isn't this kind of love what makes Mother's Day—or any day—a celebration?

"Freely you have received, freely give."
—*Matthew 10:8*

Love one another deeply, from the heart.
—1 Peter 1:22

Speaking the truth in love, we will in all things grow up into him who is the Head, that is, Christ.
—Ephesians 4:15

Ties of Love

"I led them with cords of human kindness, with ties of love."

—Hosea 11:4

> You've stepped across to
> heaven's shore
> And we are but a breath behind,
> Holding dear the truth that
> All that bound us close on earth
> Binds us still—
> For love endures forever.

My purpose is that they may be encouraged in heart and united in love, so that they may have the full riches of complete understanding. —Colossians 2:2

No one has ever seen God; but if we love one another, God lives in us and his love is made complete in us.

We know that we live in him and he in us, because he has given us of his Spirit. . . .

We love because he first loved us.

　　　　　—1 John 4:12–13, 19

All the special gifts and powers from God will someday come to an end, but love goes on forever.

　　　　　—1 Corinthians 13:8 LB

Terri

Caught Off Balance

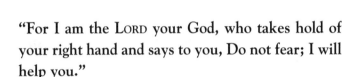

"For I am the LORD your God, who takes hold of your right hand and says to you, Do not fear; I will help you."
—Isaiah 41:13

Sudden loss, besides leaving us hurt and bewildered, can leave us listing seriously to one side. This state of imbalance is surprising, if not downright frightening. We had no idea we were leaning so heavily on a person, job, or ability until it was yanked away without warning.

When a loved one who partially defines who we are (or who we are *not*), is taken away by death, distance, divorce, or disagreement, our grief is intensified by the loss of this part of ourselves. Maybe we had depended on the person to express emotion for us or to think or decide for us. Perhaps the person was our sense of humor, our planner, our conscience, our practical side, our memory, or even our proof of worth. In one way or another, that person was our *balance*. And now we are *off* balance.

It is not just the loss of a person that can throw us off balance. Sometimes the loss of a job, ability, ideal, attribute, or goal carries with it a large chunk of our self-esteem, identity, or purpose, leaving us feeling lopsided and ready to topple over. When this happens, it may be time to confess that our sense of well-being was improperly anchored. We may also discover that our vision needs to expand— that who we are is more than what we do or how we look, and that the sum of our worth is far more than any loss.

God's secure love and His sure promise to care for us are the perfect ballast; they provide stability without adding weight to our load. When our lives are filled with Jesus Christ and the security, worth, and identity He provides, the losses we experience cannot destabilize us.

We may still toss and turn in stormy weather, but we'll never run aground or be shipwrecked.

Find rest, O my soul, in God alone; my hope comes from him. He alone is my rock and my salvation; he is my fortress, I will not be shaken. My salvation and my honor depend on God; he is my mighty rock, my refuge. Trust in him at all times, O people; pour out your hearts to him, for God is our refuge.

—Psalm 62:5–8

I waited patiently for the L*ORD*; *he turned to me and heard my cry. He lifted me out of the slimy pit, out of the mud and mire; he set my feet on a rock and gave me a firm place to stand. He put a new song in my mouth, a hymn of praise to our God. Many will see and fear and put their trust in the* L*ORD*. *Blessed is the man who makes the* L*ORD his trust, who does not look to the proud, to those who turn aside to false gods.*

—Psalm 40:1–4

In Deep Shadow

We look for light, but all is darkness; for bright-ness, but we walk in deep shadows.
—Isaiah 59:9

Dear child of God,
when clouds descend,
when depression wraps its
heavy cloak about your soul,
when God seems distant and
you, so alone—
stretch out a finger of faith,
for you may be closer than you've
ever been . . .
He may be hiding you in the
shadow of His wing.
Beneath God's wing
deep shadow blocks our sight
and bids us hear our

darkest feelings whisper
their pain, loss, and unmet needs
into the sufficiency of God's love.

He who dwells in the shelter of the Most High will rest in
the shadow of the Almighty. I will say of the LORD, "He
is my refuge and my fortress, my God, in whom I trust."
Surely he will save you from the fowler's snare and from
the deadly pestilence. He will cover you with his feathers,
and under his wings you will find refuge; his faithfulness
will be your shield and rampart. You will not fear the ter-
ror of night, nor the arrow that flies by day, nor the pes-
tilence that stalks in the darkness, nor the plague that
destroys at midday. . . .

"Because he loves me," says the LORD, "I will rescue
him; I will protect him, for he acknowledges my name.
He will call upon me, and I will answer him; I will be
with him in trouble, I will deliver him and honor him.
With long life will I satisfy him and show him my
salvation."

—Psalm 91:1–6, 14–16

The Unspeakable

Compassion invites the honesty that voices the unspeakable and brings healing.

I *found my little friend* hiding in a corner of the living room, kicking at the bottom of an easy chair and biting his lower lip. Clearly he had sought this lonely spot to deal with distress heavier than a three-year-old boy knew how to carry.

Kneeling beside him, I touched his shoulder. "What's the matter, Stevie?" I asked. "You seem so sad."

He turned toward the chair, covering his face with his hands, and I thought that this little one who laughed and hugged so easily was going to shut me out from his hurt. But then, with large, wet eyes, he turned and looked at me. "I'm mad with Mommy," he whispered, almost inaudibly.

"Even now my witness is in heaven; my advocate is on high. My intercessor is my friend as my eyes pour out tears to God; on behalf of a man he pleads with God as a man pleads for his friend."

—Job 16:19–21

"Therefore I will not keep silent; I will speak out in the anguish of my spirit, I will complain in the bitterness of my soul."

—Job 7:11

I cry aloud to the LORD; I lift up my voice to the LORD for mercy. I pour out my complaint before him; before him I tell my trouble.

—Psalm 142:1–2

Sitting in
Darkness

**When I sit in darkness, the LORD shall be a light
unto me.**

—Micah 7:8 KJV

*There is a place where the
   wounded soul goes to hide,
a place that cannot be reached by
   human caring,
though it nods at the effort.
   It's a dark, retractable place,
without windows and doors;
   a place where the soul would be
more alone than it has ever known
   unless Someone—
Someone able to walk through walls—
   was not already there waiting.*

Though the doors were locked, Jesus came and stood among them and said, "Peace be with you!"
—John 20:26

"Peace I leave with you; my peace I give you. I do not give to you as the world gives. Do not let your hearts be troubled and do not be afraid."
—John 14:27

"I have told you these things, so that in me you may have peace. In this world you will have trouble. But take heart! I have overcome the world."
—John 16:33

"Never will I leave you; never will I forsake you."
—Hebrews 13:5

No Simple Losses

————— ⸘𝕒⸘ —————

Sometimes it takes a long, long time before we can glean enrichment from the deprivation and suffering which has baffled and overwhelmed us.
—Mildred Tengbom

"*Sure I've suffered a loss,*" you say to yourself, "and I'll admit it's been tough. But I should be able to get through this thing by now!" And you push at yourself, impatient with your progress—or seeming lack of it.

The trouble is, while you weren't looking, this *thing* you were dealing with became these *things*. Loss is never simple.

Our newly married daughter discovered this unfortunate truth when, for reasons unknown, the cartilage in her hip degenerated. Through four surgeries and two terrible years, she didn't walk a step. Simply put, Cathy lost her mobility. But that's not all she lost. Loss has a way of hemorrhaging. It bleeds into so many areas of what we do and who we are.

At a time when Cathy was just establishing her independence, she lost it. She lost her freedom (even driving a car was impossible), her hope for the future (they were not sure she would ever walk again), and thus she also lost her confidence and sense of control over her own life. She was unable to keep her job, manage her home, carry on a normal married life, or enjoy her usual pursuits. She and her new husband lost control of their finances as medical bills and worries mounted. Rather than sharing joys and hopes, she and her husband, Wes, shared struggles, fears, and disappointments.

She was no longer certain who she was. It affected all of her relationships, plans, and activities. Constant pain, interruptions for surgeries, and ongoing uncertainty left her unable to continue her college education or plan for a family. She was at the mercy of new medical techniques.

She would recover from a pioneering surgical procedure by top specialists only to be worse off than before. After one operation, she spent six weeks at our house flat on her back in a hospital bed attached to a machine that kept her leg slowly moving. There were bedpans, sponge baths, and visiting hours in our family room. Her emotional stamina deteriorated along with her physical strength. The losses were complicated and demanding. The doctors didn't know what else to do for her.

Then her doctor heard of a new technique. It had never been used in a case exactly like hers, but it might work. She was scheduled for one more surgery. When the day came, I drove for hours through rush hour traffic after leaving the cemetery where I had just watched my mother's casket being lowered into the ground. It was a day I could never have imagined. Mom was gone, and this was to be my daughter's last hope for walking.

At three o'clock in the morning, Cathy was wheeled back into her room. The weary surgeon was optimistic. It had gone well.

Months later, and for the second time in my life, I had the joy of watching my daughter take her first struggling steps. She would still need crutches, and then a cane, for a long time. But there was hope.

Time has passed. There are still limitations, but Cathy is walking again. We are all so thankful. The passage of time, however, doesn't dim the fact that those were very difficult years—made even more difficult because during that same period Wes lost three jobs due to company shutdowns, his father was killed in an auto accident, and his mother suffered two heart attacks. Loss gangs up on us sometimes.

It takes all the distance and perspective that time can afford to find the gleanings of good amid such suffering, but they are there. We are all more patient now with the complexity of loss; we understand that adjusting and healing have their own schedule.

I have watched Cathy discover who she really is and find joy wherever it is available. Things that used to upset her no longer have the same disruptive power. She knows now what's really important. She and her precious husband have grown closer through this time that tried its best to tear them apart. They are both stronger in character and coping abilities. They know that life and love are our most treasured gifts.

Today I asked Cathy what she would tell you— what she has learned through all of this. She laughed and said, "How long is this book? My whole *attitude* is different. And I'm still learning.

"You know that I've always been strong—determined." (Yes, I know!) "But now I understand that willpower alone can't always get you what you want. I had to learn to trust. And now I find that I have such compassion for people who are hurting or in trouble. I'm not quick to blame them for their condition—I just want to find a way to help.

"And I'm so thankful for the support of my family and friends. I have hope today because people cared and helped me get back on my feet!

"For a long time I was controlled by what I no longer had. Now I am able to focus on what I *do* have and be thankful. Now I treasure every moment—every experience and person. The other day I caught myself treasuring my husband *when he was in a bad mood!*"

And what would Cathy tell you as you struggle with your loss? What would *I* say to you? Be patient with yourself. Be kind to your hurts and needs. They may reach farther than you realize. Loss, after all, is not simple.

> *Deep calls to deep in the roar of your waterfalls; all your waves and breakers have swept over me. By day the* Lord *directs his love, at night his song is with me—a prayer to the God of my life. I say to God my Rock, "Why have you forgotten me? Why must I go about mourning, oppressed by the enemy?" My bones suffer mortal agony as my foes taunt me, saying to me all day long, "Where is your God?" Why are you downcast, O my soul? Why so disturbed within me? Put your hope in God, for I will yet praise him, my Savior and my God.*
> —*Psalm 42:7–11*

Silent Prayers

Be joyful in hope, patient in affliction, faithful in prayer.

—Romans 12:12

> *Pain is a language*
> *without words—*
> *and so it is untouched*
> *by words.*
>
> *Does it help to know*
> *that my prayers for you*
> *are often wordless too?*
>
> *And shaped like tears.*

In the same way, the Spirit helps us in our weakness. We do not know what we ought to pray for, but the Spirit himself intercedes for us with groans that words cannot express. And he who searches our hearts knows the mind of the Spirit, because the Spirit intercedes for the saints in accordance with God's will.

—Romans 8:26–27

Dealing with
the Feelings

Those who submerge their feelings and those who cling to them like a child's 'cuddly' will self-destruct. We own our feelings in order to bring them to the healing light of Christ to be transformed.
—Elsa McInnes, *Shattered and Restored*

At times it can be more difficult to face the feelings that surround a loss than to deal with the loss itself. In the wake of a major crisis (such as the loss of a loved one, a career, or our health) strong feelings can sweep over us like a tidal wave—gut-wrenching sorrow, loneliness, fear, emptiness, despair, rage, worthlessness, helplessness, and hopelessness.

In the aftermath of life's more subtle losses (such as loss of trust, confidence, respect, support, or a cherished hope) these same feelings can take on the qualities of quicksand and slowly suck us into despair.

Having convinced us they are here to stay, these feelings demand our attention, frighten us with their intensity, and cloud our perspective. We wish we could deny them. Outrun them. Ignore them.

But they have the right to be heard and respected. While not the whole truth, they are nevertheless true from the perspective of our emotions, and they need to be dealt with tenderly, honestly, and in the light of God's complete truth. There are, however, some precautions to take when seeking to put the reality of God together with the reality of pain.

Elsa McInnes learned this. When her beloved husband died suddenly, she and her four children were left alone with their feelings of abandonment, fear, hurt, and anger. She tried to find comfort in God, but powerful emotions threatened to destroy her once vibrant faith.

In *Shattered and Restored* she writes:

"For weeks I would attend worship and receive the truth of God's love and grace and be encouraged by the songs of praise. I would hungrily grasp spiritual truth in the readings and sermon and my shattered picture of God would begin to re-form. Then I would walk out of worship into loneliness and emptiness. The combined anger of five hurting people and the emotional reality of grief would stand in stark contrast to the truth I perceived in worship. I tried in vain to reassemble my picture of God. There were new pieces that wouldn't fit. The rich gold of God's word clashed with the darker pieces of my grief. The shapes wouldn't fit together. There were comfortable pieces of truth I had held and worn smooth through the years which would not interlock with the jagged new pieces of pain. At times, in order to hold onto the word of life, I tried to deny the painful reality of anger and loneliness. At other times, when emotion ran strong, I responded by denying God's word because it seemed so false in light of my feelings.

"What was I to do? It was at that time that I stumbled upon this concept of twin realities in conflict ('emotional truth' and 'spiritual truth') and how important it is to own it *all* and bring *all* to the light of Christ for reconciliation. . . .

"It is a commonly held Christian teaching that if we receive the truth of God's word into our minds, then our corrected thought patterns will tow our wayward feelings into line.

"There is one basic error in that theory. It is a self-help system allowing Christ access to our minds only while we, in presumption, seek by sheer willpower to rectify our emotional imbalance. It's not willpower we need, but Christ's transforming power. . . .

"I learned not to fear strong feelings, but to allow them to surface fully, alive and kicking into the presence of Christ, and I discovered that, as Christ poured the oil of his healing on my feelings, my doubts about him also calmed."

Thank you, dear Elsa. God restored you so beautifully. That gives the rest of us great hope.

He reached down from on high and took hold of me; he drew me out of deep waters. He rescued me from my powerful enemy, from my foes, who were too strong for me. They confronted me in the day of my disaster, but the LORD *was my support. He brought me out into a spacious place; he rescued me because he delighted in me.*

—Psalm 18:16–19

Quotes taken from *Shattered and Restored* by Elsa McInnes, © 1990, Anzea Publishers, 3–5 Richmond Road, Homebush West, NSW 2140, Australia. Used by permission.

God Created Hope

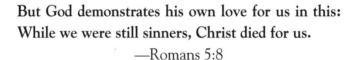

But God demonstrates his own love for us in this:
While we were still sinners, Christ died for us.
—Romans 5:8

God created our eyes—
and we looked for alternatives.
He formed our ears—
and we listened to wrong voices.
He gave us feet—
and we walked away from Him into
loss, loneliness, and despair.
So God created
A Light through the darkness—
and He is the Way.
A Promise amid lies—
and He is the Truth.
A Hope at the graveside—
and He is our Life.

But because of his great love for us, God, who is rich in mercy, made us alive with Christ even when we were dead in transgressions—it is by grace you have been saved. And God raised us up with Christ and seated us with him in the heavenly realms in Christ Jesus, in order that in the coming ages he might show the incomparable riches of his grace, expressed in his kindness to us in Christ Jesus. . . . For we are God's workmanship, created in Christ Jesus to do good works, which God prepared in advance for us to do.

—Ephesians 2:4–7, 10

Oh, God, Why?

"Why have you made me your target? . . . Why do you hide your face? . . . Why should I struggle in vain? . . . Why does the Almighty not set times for judgment? . . . Why then did you bring me out of the womb?"

—Job 7:20; 13:24; 9:29; 24:1; 10:18

I have often heard it said that people facing loss and pain should never ask why. At best, claim the critics, such questioning is counterproductive. At worst, it's a sign we're not trusting God.

Why do these people say such things? Perhaps they don't understand the question. To cry out, "Oh God, *why?*" is the natural response of a soul facing the terrible consequences of living in a sin-filled world. The knowledge that such agony was never part of God's plan for us, and thus can never seem "right," bursts from our spirit in the form of a cry that inevitably begins with *why*.

"Why am I alone now?"

"Why is my world falling apart?"

"Why have I been betrayed?"

"Why does God seem so far away when I need Him most?"

"Why did this innocent child have to suffer and die?"

"Why is life so full of pain?"

We cling to the knowledge that God has already won the victory over death. But physical—and often painful—death is still our passageway to receive the prize of eternal life and freedom from sin's ravage.

How true that God plants seeds of hope within every thorny situation. Hope, however, does not remove life's thorns and thistles. Even though we know that loss and separation cannot harm us eternally, the hurt on this earth can at times be almost unbearable.

No one understands this better than Jesus. After hanging on a cross for three hours in utter darkness, suspended by spikes through His hands and feet while the accumulated sins of humankind were heaped upon His bleeding back, our Lord cried out through parched and swollen lips, "My God, my God, *why* have you forsaken me?"

This couldn't have been a real question from One who had all wisdom and knowledge. He *knew* why. Together, He and the Father had built this terrifying moment of redemption into the foundation of the world! Yet His suffering, lonely spirit could not keep from crying out, "Why, God? *Why?* How can I bear this all alone?"

Through the tears of a loving Savior who knows the depths of what we suffer in ways we can never fathom, God hears our wrenching cries of "Oh God, *why?*"

His answers are being held tenderly in a nail-pierced hand.

What, then, shall we say in response to this? If God is for us, who can be against us? He who did not spare his own Son, but gave him up for us all—how will he not also, along with him, graciously give us all things?
    —Romans 8:31–33

For I am convinced that neither death nor life, neither angels nor demons, neither the present nor the future, nor any powers, neither height nor depth, nor anything else in all creation, will be able to separate us from the love of God that is in Christ Jesus our Lord.
    —Romans 8:38–39

Ministering Hope

The *first word* to wither and drop from the vocabulary of the discouraged is *hope*. Even if Victor Hugo was right when he said that God has written *hope* on my forehead, I'm still in trouble. Reading my own forehead is about as easy as kissing my own elbow.

Then along come those who mirror the love of God, and I see Hope reflected in their eyes. And that Hope, I discover, is not a thing but a person—Jesus Christ. They bring Christ to me through a helping hand, a word of encouragement, a message of love, and a touch that heals. Through such ministrations, they stretch my soul to receive the great Hope.

Christ always ministered like this—stretching shrunken souls with acts of love and compassion before imparting the large truth of who He was. And still today He is not content to settle back in the easy chair of our affection. Everywhere He looks, people are wounded and weary—giving up hope. He longs to go on ministering His Hope through us.

May you always be doing those good, kind things which show that you are a child of God, for this will bring much praise and glory to the Lord.
—Philippians 1:11 LB

Each one should use whatever gift he has received to serve others, faithfully administering God's grace in its various forms. If anyone speaks, he should do it as one speaking the very words of God. If anyone serves, he should do it with the strength God provides, so that in all things God may be praised through Jesus Christ.
—1 Peter 4:10–11

We have this hope as an anchor for the soul, firm and secure.
—Hebrews 6:19

Cleansing the Wound

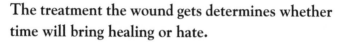

The treatment the wound gets determines whether time will bring healing or hate.

—Elsa McInnes, *Shattered and Restored*

When something of worth is taken from us, we are injured. If we lose something badly needed, highly valued, or deeply loved, the wound will be deep. If it was ripped away without warning, the laceration is jagged and raw. If it was slowly scraped away, the abrasion burns and stings.

Such wounds have one thing in common. They *hurt.* We don't like the pain, but it serves a purpose; it reminds us to treat and protect our injury. A thorough cleansing prevents serious infection, and a protective bandage shields the wound from further damage.

Emotional wounds demand the same careful attention as physical wounds, and the wounds of loss are especially vulnerable to contamination.

After the shock of losing her husband to cancer, Elsa McInnes discovered the painful truth that deep wounds can be breeding grounds for very unwelcome pests. She found that her normal and predictable emotions of sorrow, fear, and anger became infected with self-pity, blame, bitterness, and resentment. She writes:

"Lord, . . . I marvel at the gentle distinction you made as you helped me face the contamination. You never once called grief a sin. You made a distinction between sin and the emotional wound that caused it. You showed me that you bind and heal emotional wounds with deep compassion. But then you gently pointed out that you can't treat destructive attitudes that find entry through those wounds the same way. There was no point in bathing them. They needed eviction notices and since the house they resided in was mine, it rested with me to tell them they were not welcome. Lord, right then I caught an uncomfortable glimpse of the wounds I was inflicting on your Holy Spirit as you tried to bandage mine."

Elsa's words hint that we may have work to do even while we are still dealing with pain, loss, and grief. We need to remain alert and close to God lest the Enemy find opportunity in our sorrow.

We may need to forgive something that seems unforgiveable. We may need to remind ourselves of how much God has forgiven us. Forgiveness begins with a choice and continues with daily, hourly, perhaps even moment-by-moment affirmations until it stands free—until *we* stand free.

We may be required to let go with grace when the time comes; to release what is being taken from us as well as the pain the loss leaves in its place. We may have to consciously choose healing and restoration and then to verbalize what we want and need God to do for us. As we begin to express our desire to be whole and seek to obey His Word, we can rest in the truth that He knows what is best for us. He knows that we need cleansing, protection, healing, and restoration. He knows that we need *Him*.

"For I am the LORD who heals you."
—Exodus 15:26

When Jesus saw him lying there and learned that he had been in this condition for a long time, he asked him, "Do you want to get well?"
—John 5:6

Cleanse me with hyssop, and I will be clean; wash me, and I will be whiter than snow.
—Psalm 51:7

Let all who take refuge in you be glad; let them ever sing for joy. Spread your protection over them, that those who love your name may rejoice in you.

—Psalm 5:11

Quote taken from *Shattered and Restored* by Elsa McInnes, © 1990, Anzea Publishers, 3–5 Richmond Road, Homebush West, NSW 2140, Australia. Used by permission.

Saying Good-bye

Hearts don't have to stand close to join hands.

One of the most heartrending moments of life comes when close friends say good-bye, knowing that many miles will separate them from their countless shared experiences. Distance takes on the menacing look of an enemy when it dares to stand between such friends!

Soon they will be building protective shields around the ache of separation. They will feel themselves both courting and resisting the urge to clip those taut threads that bind their hearts in love. And they will argue repeatedly with a voice that warns, "Don't build new friendships—life has a demolition crew around every corner!"

But discovery lies ahead. Real friendship is resilient. The very cords that made it strong—

commitment, creativity, caring, and sharing—are elastic, and friends can remain committed and even more creative in their long-distance sharing.

Now cards and letters—stackable memories to be relived over a cup of coffee—will communicate love in indelible ink. Now calls—where the value of every word, enhanced by the coming bill—will set precious priorities and release sentiment from the soul. Anticipated visits will be far richer for their infrequency. Thoughts and feelings long saved and protected will be unlocked and shared.

Best of all, a discovery will be made that hearts in harmony can carry a lovely tune long distance.

Even though I am not physically present, I am with you in spirit.
                    —1 Corinthians 5:3

All my prayers for you are full of praise to God! When I pray for you, my heart is full of joy . . . How natural it is that I should feel as I do about you, for you have a very special place in my heart. We have shared together the blessings of God . . . Only God knows how deep is my love and longing for you—with the tenderness of Jesus Christ. My prayer for you is that you will overflow more and more with love for others, and at the same time keep on growing in spiritual knowledge and insight.
                    —Philippians 1:3–4, 7–9 LB

What Helps, What Hurts?

Wise sayings often fall on barren ground; but a kind word is never thrown away.
—Arthur Helps

Sensitivity to others often comes at considerable expense. Ask those who have lost a loved one or some important aspect of their life if they are now wiser regarding what helps and what hurts the grieving heart. They will know.

They will explain that God's love reaches out most tangibly through people who understand that

- they are not required to fix the hurt.
- curiosity is not the same as caring.
- a gentle touch can mean more than a great truth.
- God understands our questions and even our anger.
- a listening ear brings more comfort than the wisest mouth.

- people don't hurt less just because you tell them someone else hurts more.
- similar experiences give empathy but we can't know *exactly* how another person feels.
- people who add practical help to their prayers are an answer to prayer.
- words of love are words of encouragement.
- small acts of kindness are not small.
- all of the Scripture we know may not need to be quoted right now.
- losing one's balance is not the same as losing one's testimony.
- it takes time to live our questions all the way through to God's answers.
- time alone has no power to heal—God alone does.

Therefore, as God's chosen people, holy and dearly loved, clothe yourselves with compassion, kindness, humility, gentleness and patience. . . . And over all these virtues put on love, which binds them all together in perfect unity.
                              —Colossians 3:12, 14

Carry each other's burdens, and in this way you will fulfill the law of Christ.
                              —Galatians 6:2

Blessed is [s]he who is kind to the needy.
                              —Proverbs 14:21

When Hope
Is Crushed

———— ❧ ————

Losing hope, painful as it may seem, is the way to discover hope.

—David Augsburger, *When Enough Is Enough*

As *we stood chatting* after a meeting, a beautifully dressed woman of about fifty told me how deeply she was hurting. She hadn't known life could be so painful.

Until recently life had gone pretty much according to her plan. In fact, she had never been able to understand people who couldn't make life turn out right. She had met and married the perfect man, had sons who would make anyone proud, kept up a lovely home, attended church every Sunday, and found a nice job when the kids were grown. She had the formula: Live right and God will bless you with this kind of life. There was little she hoped for—except that life would continue to be this comfortable.

But it didn't. The bottom dropped out of her life and landed hard, crushing her hope for a perfect, pain-free existence.

When hope shatters, no matter how unrealistic it was, we become vulnerable to dangerous new hopes. For example, we may start to hope that, at the very least, we can rise above the pain. Isn't that what victorious living is all about? After all, God promised that we shall "mount up with wings like eagles" (Isaiah 40:31 LB).

But life may clip the wings of even that hope, forcing us to walk the pathway covered by splinters of crushed hope. Soon our feet are sore and bleeding. At this point some folks, unable to see an end to the pathway of pain, settle for a scaled-down version of hope—a prescription that promises relief for inflamed feet. This hope expects relief—demands it in fact, reasoning that it's the very least God could do. This hope has been known to plan, scheme, bargain, demand, and even use Scripture out of context in an effort to twist the arm of God. This hope leads directly to disillusionment.

True hope focuses not on plans and prescriptions but on the person of God.

This living hope takes root in the reality of pain and holds us close to our Father who "did not spare his own Son, but gave him up for us all" (Romans 8:32).

This honest hope keeps its eyes wide open and its feet firmly planted in God's unfailing promises. All of them.

This patient hope does not demand to soar; it gratefully settles for "walking without fainting."

This sustaining hope opens the door to God's healing for my hurt, God's purpose through my pain, God's rest in my struggle, God's Word for my questions, and God's peace in the midst of my storm.

This eternal hope leads directly to heaven.

False hope expects to find relief *from* suffering. True hope expects to find God *in* suffering.

And hope does not disappoint us, because God has poured out his love into our hearts by the Holy Spirit, whom he has given us.
—*Romans 5:5*

Let us draw near to God with a sincere heart in full assurance of faith, having our hearts sprinkled to cleanse us from a guilty conscience and having our bodies washed with pure water. Let us hold unswervingly to the hope we profess, for he who promised is faithful.
—*Hebrews 10:22–23*

So do not throw away your confidence; it will be richly rewarded. You need to persevere so that when you have

done the will of God, you will receive what he has promised.
—Hebrews 10:35–36

May the God of hope fill you with all joy and peace as you trust in him, so that you may overflow with hope by the power of the Holy Spirit.
—Romans 15:13

As the Calendar Turns

**My birthdays are coming so fast I feel like standing
back so I don't get run over by the calendar.**
—Stacy E. Finefrock (my Dad)

A *wise old woman* once chided me for bemoaning my
first gray hairs. (This, unfortunately, is not a recent
story.) "Honey," she said, "don't complain about gray
hairs. Turning gray is the only part of aging that
doesn't hurt!"

Another time I overheard a stooped old gentle-
man talking with a friend. "When I was a boy I used
to wonder why old men leaned over like this when
they walked," he said. "Now I know. If you try to
stand up straight, you just go on over backwards!"

These people weren't comedians; they were
sages.

We can all remember the days when we actually looked forward to birthdays, eagerly counting the weeks and days until we would turn a year older. "Mama, how long till I can hold up my thumb too?" (In less figurative language, this means "When will I be *five?*") And the day after we turned 15, we were already "almost 16."

Youth celebrates each year as a credit, deferring or ignoring the debit. As the years go on, we continue to celebrate the gains and laugh at the losses. We are preoccupied with living, and that's good.

Then someone speeds up the clock. The smoke over the birthday cake barely clears before it's time to blow out the candles again. And the strains of "Happy Birthday to You" start up again while last year's verse is only half finished, like a Sunday school chorus sung in rounds.

This is when time begins whispering her not-so-subtle suggestion that we have failed to understand her. Our understanding grows, however, when we begin paying the price in our own bodies or watching parents or friends pay it in theirs. We can no longer ignore the fact that we are breaking down, wearing out, falling apart, and losing control.

The rate of deterioration seems to depend on health, heredity, and how well we have cared for ourselves. The *perceived* rate of deterioration may depend more on attitude; the ability to cover up, adjust, and compensate; and whether or not some important parts of us are growing rather than diminishing.

As the calendar pages turn with ever-increasing speed—robbing us of vigor, agility, strength, and energy; passion, endurance, stature, and health; smooth skin, thick hair, keen sight, and sharp hearing; dexterity, balance, skill, and memory—we know where to find comfort. As we follow, love, and obey our Lord, His character will grow stronger within us, blessing us with maturity, perspective, faith, wisdom, love, patience, endurance, peace, and joy, no matter how weak our bodies become. How blessed we are to have our hope built on that which time cannot take away.

But we have this treasure in jars of clay to show that this all-surpassing power is from God and not from us. . . . Therefore we do not lose heart. Though outwardly we are wasting away, yet inwardly we are being renewed day by day. For our light and momentary troubles are achieving for us an eternal glory that far outweighs them all. So we fix our eyes not on what is seen, but on what is unseen. For what is seen is temporary, but what is unseen is eternal.

Now we know that if the earthly tent we live in is destroyed, we have a building from God, an eternal house in heaven, not built by human hands. Meanwhile we groan, longing to be clothed with our heavenly dwelling, because when we are clothed, we will not be found naked. For while we are in this tent, we groan and are burdened, because we do not wish to be unclothed but to be clothed with our heavenly dwelling, so that what is mortal may be swallowed up by life. Now it is God who has made us for this very purpose and has given us the Spirit as a deposit, guaranteeing what is to come. Therefore we are always confident and know that as long as we are at home in the body we are away from the Lord. We live by faith, not by sight.

—2 *Corinthians* 4:7, 16–18; 5:1–7

Multiplied Sorrows

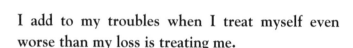

I add to my troubles when I treat myself even worse than my loss is treating me.

Left to itself, life does a fair amount of dividing and subtracting. Death and distance divide. Divorce and disagreement divide. Many treasured things are subtracted from our lives by decay, disease, deception, desertion, depravity, and the other effects of sin in this world. In spite of our best efforts, we often find ourselves on the losing end of life.

So why do we add to our own sorrows?

Unconsciously, we compare ourselves to someone who is better off, and we feel worse. Or we blame ourselves for doing what we did or for not doing what we should have done or could have done. The "if onlys" set up headquarters in our hearts. Anger boils until it hardens into resentment, bitterness, and unforgiveness. We jump to conclusions, feed negative thoughts, make assumptions, anticipate and predict the worst. And we bombard ourselves with an endless volley of depressing messages:

- I can't survive or ever be happy again without this thing/person.
- I will never get through this.
- I must be a failure/bad/hopeless.
- The rest of my life is going to be miserable.
- I have been singled out for abuse.
- I will always feel this afraid/vulnerable/angry/depressed.
- God has deserted me.
- I can't make it through one more night.
- No one can help.

If we catch ourselves in the act of saying, doing, or believing such things, we have an opportunity to tell ourselves the truth instead.

- Yes I hurt, but I will not hurt forever.
- Even pain has a beginning, a middle, and an end.
- I will survive.
- God does care.
- Some of God's people know how to comfort me.
- Even if this is my fault, beating myself won't help.
- God loves me tenderly when I'm hurting.
- I can't see it through these tears, but God does have a future for me.
- Morning will come.

Let the wise listen and add to their learning.
—Proverbs 1:5

Each of you must put off falsehood and speak truthfully.
—Ephesians 4:25

Do not add to what I command you and do not subtract from it.
—Deuteronomy 4:2

Live as children of light (for the fruit of the light consists in all goodness, righteousness and truth) and find out what pleases the Lord.
—Ephesians 5:8–10

Now may the Lord of peace himself give you peace at all times and in every way.
—2 Thessalonians 3:16

Who Betrayed Whom?

Stop trusting in man, who has but a breath in his nostrils.
—Isaiah 2:22

I looked to you, my friend,
I trusted in you and
counted on your strength,
balance, and wisdom.
I believed in you!
Because you proved human,
because you fell,
does that make you a failure?
And does it mean I have been betrayed?
Or does it simply mean that I
heaped upon your slender shoulders
the burden of idealism—
that I placed you on the pedestal of
my high standards and

chained your feet with heavy links
of expectation?
Did I ask you to be God
and then weep when you were not?

For who is God besides the LORD? And who is the Rock except our God?

—Psalm 18:31

It is better to take refuge in the LORD than to trust in man. It is better to take refuge in the LORD than to trust in princes.

—Psalm 118:8–9

"Blessed is the man who trusts in the LORD, whose confidence is in him. He will be like a tree planted by the water that sends out its roots by the stream. It does not fear when heat comes; its leaves are always green. It has no worries in a year of drought and never fails to bear fruit."

—Jeremiah 17:7–8

"For the LORD God, my God, is with you. He will not fail you or forsake you."

—1 Chronicles 28:20

The Gift of Laughter

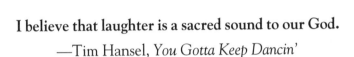

I believe that laughter is a sacred sound to our God.
—Tim Hansel, *You Gotta Keep Dancin'*

Not *all laughter* comes easily. There is a laughter that waits to be born. It is laughter at the end of exhaustion . . . laughter after pain . . . laughter for the joy of release . . . earned laughter . . . laughter all the brighter for its stark background . . . laughter stitched together with that ragged yet tough filament we call faith (or is it endurance?) . . . laughter that knows every note in the scale of life by heart—all its highs and lows—yet sings out its lilting tune anyway.

This laughter is more than just a sound, more than mirth, more than any comedian has ever hoped to evoke. It is the soul bubbling over with hope and victory. It is the voice of joy. Like a magnet it draws every scrap of life within its radius toward the promise of living, loving, and trusting.

Life does demand that we cry—often. But we need to laugh still more often. Because there will be an end to our tears, but never to our joy!

> *There is a time for everything, and a season for every activity under heaven: . . . a time to weep and a time to laugh, a time to mourn and a time to dance.*
> *—Ecclesiastes 3:1, 4*

> *"Blessed are you who weep now, for you will laugh."*
> *—Luke 6:21*

> *Those who sow in tears will reap with songs of joy. He [she] who goes out weeping, carrying seed to sow, will return with songs of joy, carrying sheaves with him [her].*
> *—Psalm 126:5–6*

Losing an Argument

You can learn many things from children. How much patience you have, for instance.
—Franklin P. Jones

One of life's most unforgettable experiences is to engage in any sort of discussion (i.e., argument) with a teenager defending his or her autonomy with the newfound weapons of reason and logic. It ranks right up there with being in a rear-end collision.

During the discussion you won't understand where you're going, and when it's over you won't know where you are or how you got there. Or why it's costing you so much money. It's worse than being audited by the IRS.

For one thing, teenagers approach discussions convinced that they hold insights discovered sometime after you last comprehended anything—if indeed you ever did. For another thing, they refuse to honor the age-old parental logic that says, "Because it's my house and that's the way I want it." Or, "Because I'm the parent and I'm paying the bills. . . ."

They say, "But wait, just *think* about it a minute," leaning heavily on the word *think* as though dangling a fresh carrot before a starving rabbit. And, "Be *reasonable*!" Which means, "No one with half a brain would disagree with me about this!"

A newly emerging adult may promise to take you on a trip from point A to point C, but en route you will inevitably pass through I-can't-believe-you-are-this-ignorant-of-the-real-issue! It is not a nice place to visit.

From my perspective, the *real* issue is how I got into this situation in the first place. I would hate to have to explain to the kid that if I were a truly logical person, I would never have become a *mother*.

But I did choose to become a mother. And as I see it, patiently loving my children through every stage, however difficult, is the way to win while seeming to lose.

How else can a logical person look at it?

"What ails you that you keep on arguing? . . ." "When will you end these speeches? Be sensible, and then we can talk. . . ." "I waited while you spoke, I listened to your

reasoning; while you were searching for words, I gave you my full attention."

—Job 16:3; 18:2; 32:11–12

The end of a matter is better than its beginning, and patience is better than pride. Do not be quickly provoked in your spirit, for anger resides in the lap of fools. Do not say, "Why were the old days better than these?" For it is not wise to ask such questions. . . . Do not pay attention to every word people say.

—Ecclesiastes 7:8–10, 21

Take note of this: Everyone should be quick to listen, slow to speak and slow to become angry, for man's anger does not bring about the righteous life that God desires.

—James 1:19–20

Above all, love each other deeply, because love covers over a multitude of sins.

—1 Peter 4:8

Puzzling over Change

Most people resist change, and yet it's the only thing that brings progress.

—From *Live and Learn and Pass It On*

If *I'm going to ponder* some great philosophical mystery, I want to pick a meaningful subject. I'd prefer not to spend my time arguing whether the chicken or the egg came first. Let somebody else figure that one out and save me the trouble. I'll work on my own puzzles.

My thorny question for this week is, Does change produce loss or does loss produce change? And if (as I strongly suspect) the answer is both, then which came first, the chicken or the egg?

I'm sorry. I shouldn't toy with a subject this serious. As necessary as change is to life and progress, it can be very difficult. Even positive change can be tough—even change that we choose.

Get married and you gain a spouse and the chance for a lifetime of love and sharing. But you lose your privacy, quite a bit of your freedom, and several arguments as well.

Have a baby and you'll be changing more than the wallpaper in what you used to call the den. You'll also change about four thousand diapers and several lofty standards. And you'll lose your heart, your sleep, and most of your hair before the kid is grown.

Move to a new house and you can lose your way to the bathroom in the night. If you relocate in a new town you lose everything from church family and friends to your favorite hamburger stand and the only person who knew how to cut your hair.

If you accept a new job, you may leave behind an annoying boss or co-worker, but you also lose your familiar position and duties.

But we don't have the luxury of choosing all of the changes that come our way. And some of the changes are frightening and difficult.

Last year my husband was among those who lost their jobs when the defense industry had to shrink to match its meager new budget. After twenty-nine years of going to work every day for the same company, Herb had nowhere to go. Our youngest had moved out just prior to Herb's layoff, so there we were, just the two of us.

There was plenty to worry about, and we could have passed the worries back and forth in an endless tournament of despair. But for some wonderful reason we didn't, opting instead to trust God and enjoy our time together. We did a lot of talking, sorting of priorities, playing, and catching up on projects around the house. God knew all of the problems and needs we were facing. He was just as aware as we were that if Herb wasn't re-hired he would lose most of his early retirement package. We decided to do what we could and leave the rest with God.

As it turned out, Herb was hired back after a couple of months, but the only job they could find for him was as a mechanical engineer. He is an *electronics* engineer. He has a master's degree in how to chase invisible electrons, not in how to repair hardware! But the company offered no schooling. Just new responsibilities and new problems.

Fortunately, my husband chooses to see change as a challenge. And what a challenge this was! He had all new jargon to learn, new concepts and new people to deal with. He was no longer in charge; he was taking orders from someone else. One day he sat at his desk looking at an elaborate sketch he had drawn while standing on the third level of a scaffold looking at the inside of a plane fuselage which was upside down and backwards. *Who drew this?* he groaned, looking at the intricate maze. *And whatever does it mean?*

But he kept at it and met the challenge, turning his losses into gains. He actually began to have fun learning and growing through it all. For while it's true that change sometimes brings loss, and loss inevitably brings change, change also brings opportunities for progress and *growth*. Or is it that growth always brings change? Sounds like a good puzzle for next week!

"Forget the former things; do not dwell on the past. See, I am doing a new thing! Now it springs up; do you not perceive it? I am making a way in the desert and streams in the wasteland . . . to give drink to my people, my chosen, the people I formed for myself that they may proclaim my praise."
—Isaiah 43:18–21

Every good and perfect gift is from above, coming down from the Father of the heavenly lights, who does not change like shifting shadows.
—James 1:17

Faith's
Last Leap

**I have fought the good fight, I have finished the
race, I have kept the faith.**
—2 Timothy 4:7

The day after my mother died, I was leafing through
her favorite daily devotional guide when I came
across a loose page torn and saved from some other
book.

Carefully removing it, I read of a young boy's
experience writing and mailing his very first letter.
Painstakingly he had printed, "Dear Grandpa," and
then spelled out what he wanted for his birthday. At
last, satisfied with the wording of his request, he put
his letter in an envelope and walked with his mother
to the mailbox. She lifted him up and said, "Let it
go." The boy hesitated. Would Grandpa really
receive the letter if he dropped it into the big, dark

box? But he did let go, and when the young boy received his grandfather's present he also received his first lesson in trust.

As I sat there I recalled my dear mother's *last* lesson in trust. I had watched her struggle between hanging on to this life and letting go of it—struggle against leaving this earth and the people she loved so dearly—repeatedly fighting her way back from the banks of the River Jordan for one more kiss, one more smile, one more touch, just one more "I love you."

It must take a lot of faith to let go when God says it is time to cross the dark chasm that separates the earthly life we know from the unknown glories beyond. It is faith's last great effort. But when we do, how swiftly faith must become sight and darkness become eternal light.

Right now, as I speculate as to the glories of heaven and the beauty of the Savior who gave Himself as a ransom for us, I can see my mother looking into His eyes. And if I know her, she's roaming through gardens of delight arm in arm with Him, exclaiming over fragrances she never dreamed existed and admiring colors that He didn't put in our rainbow.

Praise be to the God and Father of our Lord Jesus Christ!
In his great mercy he has given us new birth into a living

hope through the resurrection of Jesus Christ from the dead, and into an inheritance that can never perish, spoil or fade—kept in heaven for you, who through faith are shielded by God's power until the coming of the salvation that is ready to be revealed in the last time. In this you greatly rejoice, though now for a little while you may have had to suffer grief in all kinds of trials. These have come so that your faith—of greater worth than gold, which perishes even though refined by fire—may be proved genuine and may result in praise, glory and honor when Jesus Christ is revealed.

—1 Peter 1:3–7

He Is
Our Hope

Christ in you, the hope of glory.
—Colossians 1:27

*Sometimes the very best of life is
removed from sight and touch
and we are left behind to
cling to one another and
hope in Him Who
loved us
and gave Himself for an
eternity with
no good-byes.*

*For the Lord himself will come down from heaven, with
a loud command, with the voice of the archangel and with
the trumpet call of God, and the dead in Christ will rise
first. After that, we who are still alive and are left will be
caught up together with them in the clouds to meet the*

Lord in the air. And so we will be with the Lord forever.
Therefore encourage each other with these words.
—1 Thessalonians 4:16–18

When Christmas Isn't Welcome

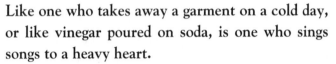

> Like one who takes away a garment on a cold day, or like vinegar poured on soda, is one who sings songs to a heavy heart.
> —Proverbs 25:20

If only holidays would have the grace to know when *not* to happen.

One brave woman I know, in spite of her staggering and relentless collection of heavy losses, went out and purchased lovely Christmas cards. She stamped and addressed them, wrote personal notes in each one, and then found she couldn't bring herself to mail them. So she tossed them all into the garbage and watched the trash collector take them away.

After a painful year it's hard to send messages of peace and good will to all. Christmas isn't welcome when it glibly promises cozy togetherness and prepackaged joy that it can't deliver. Parties and bright lights cannot dismiss the darkness of crisis, trauma, pain, and death.

And yet God sent the Light of the World into such darkness. All around there was oppression, sickness, and suffering.

Christmas wasn't welcomed then either. It was shunted into the dark corner of a dank stable. Yet the animals, along with the weary and wondering new mother and her husband, found they were not blinded by the light of His glory. He left His brilliance behind and came with a soft cry into the night. Only a lantern lit the face of God.

Had it not been for the angels and the star, no one would have guessed that God had come to earth . . . except for those who sensed the love glowing in that dark place. Christmas came amid pain and poverty, loss and loneliness.

When we can't say "Merry Christmas," perhaps we can whisper, "Welcome, Light of the World. Never has the light of your presence been more needed. Shine softly in my darkness."

"The people living in darkness have seen a great light; on those living in the land of the shadow of death a light has dawned."

—Matthew 4:16

He has sent me to bind up the brokenhearted, to proclaim freedom for the captives and release from darkness for the prisoners . . . to comfort all who mourn, and provide for those who grieve in Zion—to bestow on them a crown of beauty instead of ashes, the oil of gladness instead of mourning, and a garment of praise instead of a spirit of despair.

—Isaiah 61:1–3

"I will lead the blind by ways they have not known, along unfamiliar paths I will guide them; I will turn the darkness into light before them and make the rough places smooth. These are the things I will do; I will not forsake them."

—Isaiah 42:16

Unshared Joy

**My comfort in my suffering is this: Your promise
preserves my life.**
—Psalm 119:50

*When you were taken
so was my joy in living,
for even those things which would now
give joy
cannot be shared with you,
And there is sorrow in unshared joy.
Joy is giving and receiving.
When one is taken away who shared
in such a relationship,
the other must learn to give and receive
in other ways.
There are thoughts and events
special only to each other.*

And the emptiness of no longer sharing
turns into loneliness.
Only You can meet my loneliness, O God.
Only You know where my feet have been,
where I now stand
and where I am going.
So I trust in you
and share with you completely.
To you I give
and from you I receive.
And once again
I know the meaning of joy.

© 1991 by Marilyn K. Anglin

When my spirit grows faint within me, it is you who know my way. . . . Look to my right and see; no one is concerned for me. I have no refuge; no one cares for my life. I cry to you, O LORD; I say, "You are my refuge, my portion in the land of the living." Listen to my cry, for I am in desperate need.
—Psalm 142:3–6

My help comes from the LORD, the Maker of heaven and earth. He will not let your foot slip—he who watches over you will not slumber; indeed, he who watches over Israel will neither slumber nor sleep. The LORD watches over you—the LORD is your shade at your right hand; the sun will not harm you by day, nor the moon by night. The

LORD will keep you from all harm—he will watch over your life; the LORD will watch over your coming and going both now and forevermore.

—*Psalm 121:2–8*

Let the morning bring me word of your unfailing love, for I have put my trust in you. Show me the way I should go, for to you I lift up my soul.

—*Psalm 143:8*

The Morning of Eternity

"See, I have engraved you on the palms of my hands."
—Isaiah 49:16

Probably no clouds were more threatening than those that gathered above Christ's cross. All of creation must have rushed into mourning for the shame of it— that their Creator, the One whose hands had formed the earth and heavens, should have those hands pierced with nails by those He created.

But deep inside the clouds' darkness, lightning glory gathered, waiting to burst forth in victory, waiting to split the dark veil of sin hanging between God and His beloved creation.

Has ever such a silver lining been spoken as "It is finished"?

Perhaps only "He is risen!"

Oh, world, trace with joy the silver lining that will never tarnish. Tell it everywhere!

RISEN!

is

He!

The angel said to the women, "Do not be afraid, for I know that you are looking for Jesus, who was crucified. He is not here; he has risen, just as he said. Come and see the place where he lay. Then go quickly and tell his disciples: 'He has risen from the dead and is going ahead of you into Galilee. There you will see him.' Now I have told you."

—Matthew 28:5–7

Wise Sayings

May all the wonderful things I will say about you after you are gone be found, complete, in the thesaurus of our todays.

The grief of loss is a heavy load. Pity those who find themselves adding regret to its burden. The "if onlys" can tip the scales and unbalance us if we're not careful.

With each new day God offers us opportunities to prevent regret. *Today* we can speak encouragement and voice our feelings. If we do it now and say it now, we are practicing the wisdom of kindness.

I have long held a motto that if I think a kind thought about someone—anything at all—and do not pass it on, I am wasting diamonds. Yet, regrettably, I find I have waste cans filled with them. The kind thoughts that form in us, yet are never shaped into words or acts, may prove to be the squandering of our most valuable human resource.

Today let me tell you, my friend, that your laugh is as much fun for me as it is for you—that your tears land in my heart—that tea with you is always sweeter—that knowing you are there for me is better than owning the national treasury.

Today let me say, my child, that I see greatness in you—that I love seeing life through your eyes—that you are growing evidence of God's goodness to me—and that I sometimes look at you and congratulate myself.

Today let me tell you, my husband, that I have experienced God's tender love through you—that I'm asking God to give you a star for every back rub you've given me—that I admire the way you turn problems into challenges—and that your steady, faithful character is the most beautiful love letter ever written.

Today let me tell you, my heavenly Father, that I am rich because of You—that I stand in awe of Your creativity every time I give You one of my tangled messes—that You are altogether beautiful—and that I love the family You are building for Yourself. Thank you for letting me be part of it!

A word aptly spoken is like apples of gold in settings of silver.
—Proverbs 25:11

A wise man's heart guides his mouth, and his lips promote instruction. Pleasant words are a honeycomb, sweet to the soul and healing to the bones.
—Proverbs 16:23–24

From the fruit of his lips a man is filled with good things as surely as the work of his hands rewards him.
—Proverbs 12:14

A Friend
in Need

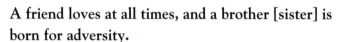

**A friend loves at all times, and a brother [sister] is
born for adversity.**
—Proverbs 17:17

Friendship gives a license to show up at the door of need
without asking "When would you like me to come?"
or "What would you like me to do?" Friendship does
not call out, "Just let me know if you need anything."
True friendship whispers, "I'm here," and, with sensitivity, respect, and understanding, promptly steps
through the door.

But what about honoring the right to invite?
Those who wait for parchment invitations wait long,
for need rarely throws a party—rarely even has a
voice.

Yet need has its own needs. It needs protection
from strangers who tromp in with work boots and

good intentions. And it needs relief from acquaintances wearing the spiked heels of advice and pat answers.

Need waits with longing for the entrance of dear ones who, on ordinary days, pad barefoot through the soul.

"Oh, that I had someone to hear me!"
—Job 31:35

"A despairing man [or woman] should have the devotion of his friends, even though he [she] forsakes the fear of the Almighty."
—Job 6:14

The Lift
of Music

When words leave off, music begins.
—Heinrich Heine

Living can be a hard business. It can strip away our resources. We can lose confidence, patience, perspective, and even our sense of humor. When this
happens we urgently need to find those gifts with the
power to rejuvenate.

God hides these spirit-lifters everywhere—in His
nature, in His Word, in prayer, in someone's arms, in
a healthy cry or a hearty laugh. But for unparalleled
restorative power, music is hard to beat. It seems to
be the heart's native tongue.

How often I have sat cross-legged between the
speakers of my stereo, singing or just letting harmony
wrap itself around my wounds and weariness. How
often I have dragged myself to a rehearsal or perfor-

mance and later skipped away restored. How often I have joined other voices in worship and praise and been lifted into the presence of God. Music has power to elevate, speak, soothe, teach, touch, energize, and unify.

Melody adds wings to words and flies them over obstacles that stand in the way of understanding. Within its measures music carries a large measure of comprehension. Somehow we can believe love that serenades us. Somehow we can hear hope that sings to us in the dark.

Yet even if music could do none of these things, it would still give soaring voice to our praise. And as we lift songs of worship we too will be lifted. That's the promise of praise.

Declare the praises of him who called you out of darkness into his wonderful light.
—1 Peter 2:9

Sing for joy to God our strength; shout aloud to the God of Jacob! Begin the music, strike the tambourine, play the melodious harp and lyre.
—Psalm 81:1–2

Pain

He has seen but half the universe who never has been shewn the house of Pain.
—Ralph Waldo Emerson

My life is
Your song, dear Lord,
And if You choose to
write that song,
in part,
in minor key,
give voice to sing despite
the taste of tears.
With hands hard-clasped
in pain,
and head bowed low
in trust,

I know You hear such
minor songs
as major praise.

My eyes are ever on the LORD, for only he will release my feet from the snare. Turn to me and be gracious to me, for I am lonely and afflicted. The troubles of my heart have multiplied; free me from my anguish.

—Psalm 25:15–17

Be merciful to me, O LORD, for I am in distress; my eyes grow weak with sorrow, my soul and my body with grief. . . . But I trust in you, O LORD; I say, "You are my God." My times are in your hands.

—Psalm 31:9, 14–15

The LORD is my strength and my shield; my heart trusts in him, and I am helped. My heart leaps for joy and I will give thanks to him in song.

—Psalm 28:7

Resurrecting
Dreams

The word of God is living and active. Sharper than any double-edged sword, it penetrates even to dividing soul and spirit, joints and marrow; it judges the thoughts and attitudes of the heart. Nothing in all creation is hidden from God's sight. Everything is uncovered and laid bare before the eyes of him to whom we must give account.

—Hebrews 4:12–13

The Lord has a way of looking into the very heart of things—especially the human heart. And there's no use trying to hide what's there.

One day I came to His Word with a nameless ache tucked away inside, troubling me, as it had been for several days. I read Luke's account of Jesus entering the town of Nain, where He came upon a heartbroken widow following the coffin of her only son.

When the Lord saw her, his heart went out to her, and he said, "Don't cry." Then he went up and touched the coffin, and those carrying it stood still. He said, "Young man, I say to you, get up!" The dead man sat up and began to talk, and Jesus gave him back to his mother (Luke 7:11–15).

As I pondered what this story could possibly have to do with me, the Lord looked into my heart and said, "Something has died in you, Susan. What is this thing you're mourning and carrying in a coffin?"

I was startled, for I hadn't known that a funeral was going on inside me. But He reached out and touched the coffin that I was indeed laboring beneath, and I finally stood still and looked.

An important dream was being taken for burial—a dream the Lord knew I needed to have alive.

Very quietly, from within the depths of me, I heard Jesus whisper, "Do you suppose that if I can resurrect people, I can resurrect dreams too?"

I read the story again and saw the compassion, the power, and the *truth*. When our last hope is being taken for burial, Jesus sees, wipes away the tears of sorrow, and speaks LIFE into our emptiness.

Praise God, He is the Lord of resurrection! The Lord of hope! In choosing Jesus as Savior and Lord, we have chosen abundant, eternal life. And it starts in *this* world.

I have set before you life and death, blessings and curses. Now choose life, so that you and your children may live and that you may love the LORD your God, listen to his voice, and hold fast to him. For the LORD is your life.
—*Deuteronomy 30:19–20*

One Brief Burst of Glory

Heaven gives its favorites early death.
—George Gordon

Like an annual flower
  she blossomed
in one brief burst of glory,
  dazzling eye and heart.
Designed by her Creator
  for one treasured season of
joy and inspiration—
  then gone—
never needing to know
  sharp pruning shears
nor harsh, barren winters
  and painful, repeated struggles
up through frozen sod to
  gray and weeping skies,
as we perennials must.

*Precious in the sight of the L*ORD *is the death of his saints.*
—*Psalm 116:15*

A Harvest of Thanksgiving

Was anything real ever gained without sacrifice of some kind?

—Arthur Helps

Our Pilgrim parents came to this continent looking for a land where they could live and worship in freedom. They were met with hardship, stark poverty, sickness, despair, and loss upon loss as they were pitted against hostile nature.

A combination of exposure, over-exertion, and inadequate provisions claimed one brave life after another. Their records show that by March 1621 half of their remaining hundred had died, "the living scarcely able to bury the dead."

Yet one by one they carried their precious ones to a field at the summit of a small cliff and buried them there—thirteen of the eighteen wives, more than half of the fathers, four entire families.

Realizing that the Indians must never know the extent of their losses, they did not mark the graves with even a small stone. Instead they planted their grave-field with corn.

We do not suffer as profoundly as our Pilgrim parents, yet we are still afflicted. We too have lost things precious to us—people, health, hopes, abilities, dreams for ourselves and for our children. But instead of planting something of use or beauty over the graves of our losses, some of us have built monuments instead, making it easy for our Enemy to target our areas of vulnerability.

Can we be as brave as our ancestors and baffle the Enemy by refusing to mark the graves of our losses? More than that, dare we convert our cemeteries to cornfields?

Ah, that we may learn to yield a harvest of Thanksgiving from the ground of our losses! It is our rich heritage.

Remember your leaders. . . . Consider the outcome of their way of life and imitate their faith. Jesus Christ is the same yesterday and today and forever. . . . Through Jesus, therefore, let us continually offer to God a sacrifice of praise—the fruit of lips that confess his name.
—Hebrews 13:7–8, 15

"I tell you the truth, unless a kernel of wheat falls to the ground and dies, it remains only a single seed. But if it dies, it produces many seeds."

—John 12:24

A Tribute to Living

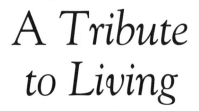

Some die without having lived; others live, though they have already died.
—Unknown

To My *Dear Pastor Hart,*

I'm forwarding this letter to your heavenly address. Even though you are gone, I need to tell you some things. I want you to know the most important lessons you taught me, both from the pulpit and from your life.

You proved to me that life is best lived in precise, declarative sentences of truth. That such truth delivers best when it is both simple and profound. That truth belabored is truth belittled. I experienced the impact of this truth as you mixed it with humor, enthusiasm, love, commitment, and full knowledge of its authority.

I watched you prove that people, God's Word, and His presence, praise, and love are the only important and lasting things on this earth.

I watched you savor and enjoy all that God brought to you while you were here. I have never known anyone more fully alive while confined to the limitations of humanity and this world.

But God has taken you home now, where you are truly alive. He has left me here. I will carry on.

You left rich resources for the task, for I've not only been taught but also touched and changed by you. I feel the stinging truth that life is short. I feel the prodding truth that my world will not be changed unless I spend myself as you did.

You were a good steward of your *life*—you spent it for the glory of God. I, in turn, will try to be a good steward of your *death*, spending its opportunities for the glory of God.

But I can't help missing you. I'm not ashamed of my tears. I'm so grateful that I told you, just two days before you left us so unexpectedly, that I love you and thank God for bringing you to us. You responded by telling me how much you loved me—loved us all—and how thankful you were that you came here.

You did, indeed, love us. How well named you were. You both lived and died with heart. God gave us His best in you. We'll not waste His generous gift.

Eternal love in Christ,
Susan

Written on the death of my pastor, Hartley Christenson, who suffered a massive heart attack while playing tennis on September 7, 1985, at the age of 49. This book is dedicated in part to his wife and my friend, Marlene.

"He has crossed over from death to life."
—John 5:24

And I heard a loud voice from the throne saying, "Now the dwelling of God is with men, and he will live with them. They will be his people, and God himself will be with them and be their God. He will wipe every tear from their eyes. There will be no more death or mourning or crying or pain, for the old order of things has passed away."
—Revelation 21:3–4

Creative Healing

Within every furrow of grief lies a seed of healing.

The holidays just weren't going to be the same without my mother around. She had loved the season so much—the music, the meaning, the decorations, and our family gatherings. I had no idea how I was going to get through them without her.

But then an idea came to me. I don't know exactly when or how it came, but it arrived with an urgency I could not ignore. I had to make a special "Mom Tree."

Never mind that I had a hundred and one things to accomplish before Christmas. Never mind that we already had a fully decorated ten-foot pine in our living room. Never mind that I didn't want even that *one* Christmas tree, let alone *two*.

Yet the thought persisted. Get another tree especially for Mom. Decorate it with her collection of white angels, pink cherubs, and the little white lace fans she had adorned with flowers. Use tiny white lights, a garland of silver ribbon, tuck airy bunches of dried baby's breath into the branches, and make special ornaments.

Make special ornaments? I didn't have time to take a deep breath! How could I take time to shop for materials and design ornaments?

But an out-of-town friend called to ask a favor. They needed trees and decorations for their academy's big holiday outreach program. Would I check out a discount Christmas warehouse near the Mexican border?

The warehouse didn't have what my friend needed, but, as it turned out, they were practically giving away pearl-white balls, silver ribbon, small peach and pink silk roses, and strands of tiny pearls. The ornaments made themselves in my head. They were beautiful. I could see them hanging on the tree that somehow "had to be."

So I let other things go undone and I made ornaments. I thought about my Mom as I worked—the things she loved, said, and did, ways in which we were alike, ways in which we were different. It seemed we were creating the tree together, for her handiwork and mine hung there side by side. She was, after all, here for Christmas.

Night after night I would stay downstairs after everyone had gone to bed and just sit looking at our beautiful tree—feeling, remembering, letting go, and taking hold. Sometimes I cried, sometimes I smiled. Sometimes I felt Mom was enjoying it too. And then I would laugh at myself, thinking how drab my wonderful tree must look next to heaven's splendor. But it was good. For I was taking time to grieve—creatively.

I would never have thought of such an idea myself, but the One who created us in His image knows how to lead us into experiences that will help us work through loss. Perhaps we will find comfort in working on a special garden, scrapbook, videotape, memory quilt, afghan in his or her favorite colors, or a special song, painting, or poem.

But however we work through our sorrow, we can rest in the knowledge that our great Creator offers us the comfort of creative healing, for He is in the center of our sorrow.

As a mother comforts her child, so will I comfort you.
—Isaiah 66:13

I have put my words in your mouth and covered you with the shadow of my hand—I who set the heavens in place, who laid the foundations of the earth . . . Sorrow and sighing will flee away. I, even I, am he who comforts you.

—*Isaiah 51:16, 11–12*

He Comes in Winter

Oh, that you would rend the heavens and come down!
—Isaiah 64:1

He could have come in
  springtime
    when flowers force their way
  through sod and
    bleating hope is born.
He could have been spring's Lamb!

He could have come in
  summer
    when sun streams down
  to warm that hope and
    breezes cool the doubts.
Ho, summer's Brightest Son!

He could have come in
autumn
when hope flames forth
with blazing joy and
crimson paints the earth.
Behold, He's autumn's Glory!

But He comes in
winter
when hope lies frozen
in the night and
blizzards rake our souls.
He comes, our Living Hope!

You see, at just the right time, when we were still powerless, Christ died for the ungodly. Very rarely will anyone
die for a righteous man, though for a good man someone
might possibly dare to die. But God demonstrates his own
love for us in this: While we were still sinners, Christ died
for us. . . . For if, when we were God's enemies, we
were reconciled to him through the death of his Son, how
much more, having been reconciled, shall we be saved
through his life!

—Romans 5:6–8, 10

"I have come that they may have life, and have it to the
full."

—John 10:10

No Rain, No Gain

Growing Through
Life's Storms

Treasures of Darkness

Ye fearful saints, fresh courage take, the clouds ye so much dread are big with mercy, and shall break in blessings on your head.
—William Cowper

Within the depths of
His darkest clouds
God often seems to bury His
richest treasures—
    silver streaks of growth,
    sterling faith,
    precious, gleaming truths—
for His beloved children.
Has a dense cloud of
    doubt,
    pain,
    loss,
    trouble,

frustration or
loneliness
settled over you, dear one?
Search out the treasures of darkness!
The riches of your Heavenly Father hide there—
with your name engraved in silver!

I will give you the treasures of darkness, riches stored in
secret places, so that you may know that I am the LORD,
the God of Israel who calls you by name.
—Isaiah 45:3

From now on I will tell you of new things, of hidden
things unknown to you. They are created now and not
long ago; you have not heard of them before today.
—Isaiah 48:6–7

I am the LORD, and there is no other; apart from me
there is no God. I will strengthen you, though you have
not acknowledged me, so that from the rising of the sun
to the place of its setting men may know there is none besides me. I am the LORD, and there is no other. I form
the light and create darkness, I bring prosperity and create disaster; I, the LORD, do all these things. . . . Turn
to me and be saved, all you ends of the earth; for I am
God, and there is no other. They will say of me, "In the
LORD alone are righteousness and strength."
—Isaiah 45:5–7, 22, 24

Growing Pains

Growing up isn't for sissies.

—Mary Betcher

The difficult truth about truth is that it often requires us to change our perspectives, attitudes, and rules for living.

Change of any sort is seldom easy. And change that produces personal growth is never easy. Yet as we submit to the One who never changes, He marvelously works in our lives.

I have a friend rich in the determination to grow. She is rich too in opportunities, for life dealt her a crushing load—one that offered only two choices: "fight" or "fold." She chose to fight, and invited me to join her.

As I walked with this friend through her struggles, I occasionally heard her wail, "Please, Lord, I don't want to grow anymore!"

But I knew she didn't really mean it. Other than unscheduled retreats beneath the covers of her bed for tears and talk with the Lord, she never stopped enlarging the house of her spirit.

I have watched her work at rebuilding the losses of her incredibly painful childhood and early adulthood. Continually she seeks to know and be known, love and be loved. Step by step she is living out the life-changing truth of God's redemptive love and power.

With joy I've seen her discover her worth and move into her potential in Christ. Over and over she has let go of her own pain to get on with the business of living and of serving others who are hurting.

It is only the discomfort of such continuous stretching that my friend bemoans. And I can't blame her, for growing pains are real.

Neither do I blame her for not fully appreciating her progress, for she doesn't have the beautiful view of the results that I have. I hope, though, that she can hear applause in my words and feel approval in my love. Because growing up in Christ is surely the most difficult, courageous, exhilarating, and eternally important work any of us will ever do.

Speaking the truth in love, we will in all things grow up into him who is the Head, that is, Christ.

—Ephesians 4:15

His divine power has given us everything we need for life and godliness through our knowledge of him who called us by his own glory and goodness. Through these he has given us his very great and precious promises, so that through them you may participate in the divine nature and escape the corruption in the world caused by evil desires.

But grow in the grace and knowledge of our Lord and Savior Jesus Christ. To him be glory both now and forever! Amen.

—2 Peter 1:3–4; 3:18

Grow Up to Be a Child

. . . and a little child will lead them, . . .
—Isaiah 11:6

Almighty God squeezed Himself tight
and became a little child.
Then He Who satisfies every living thing
fed His hunger at a woman's breast.
He Who never slumbers or sleeps
learned to sleep through the night.
He Who spoke all creation into being
learned to say, "please" and "thank you."
He Who made countless galaxies learned to count to ten.
And then He said,
Unless you, too, become like a little child,
you cannot enter the kingdom of heaven.

God's kingdom is confusing by this world's standards. To have life, we must give it away. To rule, we must serve. To grow up, we must become like a little child.

We came into this world as children—full of curiosity, wonder, creativity, honesty, openness, humility, confidence, simplicity, and trust. But blow by crushing blow this sinful world taught us to stop trusting and convinced us to start hiding ourselves away and to lie about our needs or use our creativity to meet them in wrong ways.

God came to us as a little child so that He could teach us to go back and become little children with an all-wise, all-powerful, constantly loving, and perfect Heavenly Father. Christ came to reclaim the children that sin stole away. It is safe to grow up in Him.

At that time the disciples came to Jesus and asked, "Who is the greatest in the kingdom of heaven?" He called a little child and had him stand among them. And he said: "I tell you the truth, unless you change and become like little children, you will never enter the kingdom of heaven. Therefore, whoever humbles himself like this child is the greatest in the kingdom of heaven. And whoever welcomes a little child like this in my name welcomes me."
—Matthew 18:1–5

To all who received him, to those who believed in his name, he gave the right to become children of God—

children born not of natural descent, nor of human deci-
sion or a husband's will, but born of God. The Word
became flesh and made his dwelling among us. We have
seen his glory, the glory of the One and Only, who came
from the Father, full of grace and truth.

—John 1:12–14

The Success of Failure

We all stumble in many ways.
—James 3:2

Some of life's clouds stay high above us and merely threaten. Some sprinkle or mist, and some pour torrents. Others seem to move right down to where we live, settle over us, and dim our view of who we are and what we can do.

One such cloud is the leaden fog bank of personal failure. It covers our souls like a damp blanket, depressing us and obscuring our judgment. Soon we are in danger of believing not simply that we have failed but that we are a *failure*. What a difference between the two!

To have *failed* is to have lived, tried, and been proven to be imperfect like everyone else. To have failed is to own more wisdom, understanding, and experience than do those who sit on life's sidelines playing it safe. To have failed is to claim a clearer knowledge of what not to do the next time. And to have failed is to have an opportunity to extend to ourselves the grace that God so freely extends to us.

We become a *failure* when we allow mistakes to take away our ability to learn, give, grow, and try again. We become a failure if we allow our transgressions to activate an internal voice of eternal self-blame and shame. We become a failure if we let the "shoulds" and the "if onlys" suck us into their mire. And we are a failure when we become content with failing.

The mire caused by our blunders, errors, and failings can become the quicksand that traps us in regret, or it can become the material we use to make building blocks of righteousness. God waits to give us another chance. His grace is well spent on fresh starts.

Cast your cares on the LORD and he will sustain you; he will never let the righteous fall.
—Psalm 55:22

If the LORD delights in a man's way, he makes his steps firm; though he stumble, he will not fall, for the LORD upholds him with his hand.
—Psalm 37:23–24

The LORD upholds all those who fall and lifts up all who are bowed down.

—Psalm 145:14

To him who is able to keep you from falling and to present you before his glorious presence without fault and with great joy—to the only God our Savior be glory, majesty, power and authority, through Jesus Christ our Lord, before all ages, now and forevermore! Amen.

—Jude 24–25

Feeling Insignificant

What awe,
what wonder,
for tiny man on
frail earth
to realize that
size
is no measure of
worth
in God's enormous eyes.

One of Satan's most effective ploys is to make us believe that we are small, insignificant, and worthless. And it's often a fairly easy job for him, for as we measure our small lives and sin-shriveled souls against the vast holiness of God, we realize that indeed we are insignificant!

But God's enemy deceives us by suggesting that this realistic assessment of ourselves, this appropriate, honest *humility* is actually *humiliation*. Such truth-twisting tactics keep us so low, so filled with shame that we can't begin to see ourselves as God has chosen to see us.

To view ourselves through our Creator's loving, tear-filled eyes, we need to climb Calvary's hill and look down from the cross of Christ—for that is where God declared that we are worth the life of His precious Son.

Such a holy, awesome sacrifice of love bestows inestimable worth to us, His beloved in Christ.

Ephesians 1:4–8 tells us that God "*chose us* in him before the creation of the world to be *holy and blameless* in his sight. In *love* he predestined us to be adopted as *sons* (and *daughters*) through Jesus Christ, in accordance with his *pleasure* and *will*—to the praise of his *glorious grace*, which he has *freely* given us in the One he loves. In him we have *redemption* through his blood, the *forgiveness of sins*, in accordance with the *riches* of God's grace that he *lavished* on us with all wisdom and understanding" (emphasis mine).

He also declares that He has not just sprinkled, but has "*poured out* His love into our hearts by the Holy Spirit whom he has given us" (Romans 5:5).

We are the temple of God. We have been bought at great price. And we are instructed to honor God with our bodies (1 Corinthians 6:19–20). How God honors us by His indwelling presence and love!

> When I consider your heavens, the work of your fingers, the moon and the stars, which you have set in place, what is man that you are mindful of him, the son of man that you care for him? You made him a little lower than the heavenly beings and crowned him with glory and honor. You made him ruler over the works of your hands; you put everything under his feet . . . O LORD, our LORD, how majestic is your name in all the earth!
>
> —Psalm 8:3–9

> "Do not be afraid, little flock, for your Father has been pleased to give you the kingdom."
>
> —Luke 12:32

This Isn't Funny Anymore

The workshop of character is everyday life.
—Maltbie D. Babcock

The *four of us* stood in the blazing sun amid sagebrush and roadside dust watching our car spew forth its heated opinion about our forcing it to climb mountain roads at its age. Any hope of making it to our niece's wedding on time seemed to be going up in smoke too.

My husband, Herb, and our officially ASE certified "World Class Auto Technician" son, Jeff, wore the look men wear when they know exactly what's happening but can't do a thing about it. My daughter-in-law, Margie, and I wore the look women wear when they see their husbands look like that but can't do a thing about it.

Herb was supposed to be videotaping the wedding. Margie had agreed to coordinate the proceedings. I had promised to help my sister with last-minute details. And Jeff was to be one of the groomsmen; yet there he stood in shorts and sandals, poking around under the hood, making solemn pronouncements. "Looks like cooling system vapor lock. This car's going to need considerable time to cool off, a gallon or two of water, and some serious attention later."

We could have used a similar prescription. This wasn't just a bad day we were having; it was a "last straw" day. A sense of humor seemed way beyond my emotional reach, so I settled for a sense of balance.

"Just don't make things worse," I kept saying to myself. "Remain calm. If you can't say something good, try to focus on what needs to be done." So, as cars and trucks zoomed by, intent on reaching their destinations, I stood by the car, its hood raised like a huge flag, and prayed for a solution.

Finally a knight in a shining white pick-up truck pulled over and offered assistance. He left with our name, location, and my sister's phone number, promising to call for help as soon as he reached town. At least she would know what had happened to us.

Several minutes later my brother and his family, on their way to the ceremony, rescued us in time to intercept the man my sister had dispatched after hearing of our plight.

At the wedding site we stuffed our unhappy bodies into suits and ties, dresses and pantyhose. We weren't the only ones feeling the heat, for the plea came, "Could you please take ice water to the thirsty bridal party?"

Thankful that I had arrived in time to help a little, I hurried to gather a pitcher of water and cups. Hands full, I kicked the screen door open only to have it slam back into the pitcher, sending a cascade of water down my face and dress. They drank what was left, I dried what I could.

In spite of delays, the wedding commenced. The bride was radiant—the groom nervous and tender—the minister (the bride's stepfather) touching and genuine in his expressions of his love for them and for God. I passed tissues to my sister, my daughter, and my daughter-in-law. It's good to have experience in these matters.

After the reception, the guys headed down the mountain. They watered the car and talked severely to it, but, unheeding, it stranded us again on the way home—this time on a desolate patch of freeway between someplace and someplace else. Our daughter and son-in-law were following us, however, so at least we had help available.

On the way to the gas station, the girls bubbled with annoying good cheer. This was a family adventure, they said. We were making a memory that we would surely talk and laugh about later.

They found a huge white enameled cooking pot in the trunk of our daughter's car and filled it with water for the radiator.

Herb rode in the passenger seat dangling the pot from his thumbs, solemnly explaining (as engineers tend to do) that he was demonstrating the highly effective "decoupling theory" to prevent sloshing and spills.

The girls were certain that this was fun.

I was certain that we didn't need this much fun.

I was tired. Exhausted, really. And nothing was very funny. The day had topped off a bad week, which had followed an even worse one, after an unbelievable month which pretty much matched the whole year.

When life's heavy storms come like that, one after another, you can find yourself reeling, staggering, going to your knees, adjusting, being knocked flat again, then struggling up in time to catch yet another blow.

The accumulated losses can become so overwhelming that it takes only the sprinkles of life's daily problems to tip your boat. Every distress feels like a disaster. Nothing looks like a simple aggravation that could, with a little perspective and humor, be turned into an adventure.

When I've lost my sense of humor, when I can no longer bend and flex with the day's stresses and distresses, I don't need to give my day or my attitude over to the Lord. I need to give myself to Him. If I hope to grow through life's sprinkles as well as its downpours, if I want to learn patience and perseverance and gain heavenly perspective, I need to hide in Him. Rest in Him. Find myself renewed in Him. He waits with healing in His wings.

> Yet the LORD longs to be gracious to you; he rises to show you compassion. For the LORD is a God of justice. Blessed are all who wait for him! . . . How gracious he will be when you cry for help! As soon as he hears, he will answer you. Although the LORD gives you the bread of adversity and the water of affliction, your teachers will be hidden no more, with your own eyes you will see them. Whether you turn to the right or to the left, your ears will hear a voice behind you, saying, "This is the way; walk in it." . . . He will also send you rain for the seed you sow in the ground, and the food that comes from the land will be rich and plentiful.
>
> —Isaiah 30:18–21, 23

> But for you who fear my name, the sun of righteousness will rise with healing in his wings. And you will go free, leaping with joy like calves let out to pasture.
>
> —Malachi 4:2 LB

Don't Give Up

By perseverance the snails reached the ark.
—Charles Haddon Spurgeon

We're *slow-brew* Christians in an instant world. Small wonder that we get discouraged with ourselves!

The world serves up instant food, instant entertainment, and instant credit. We're offered computers, fax machines, microwave ovens, automatic phone dialers, remote control televisions, Polaroid cameras, high-speed elevators, and quick copy machines. We reach for hot-line help, rapid-rise yeast, express mail, and automatic banking. We can travel in racy cars with high-octane fuel, supersonic jets, and even orbit the globe in space capsules.

Then comes the Christian, a foot soldier on a straight and narrow path. "Follow Me," Jesus says. "Put one foot in front of the other in moment-to-moment obedience." (Nothing like an invitation to take a stroll on the freeway!)

Then Jesus tells us that if we follow Him, He'll make us "fishers of men" (Mark 1:17). What? Bait and wait? Mend and cast nets? Clean and preserve the catch? (An unattractive assignment with flash-frozen fish fillet in the local supermarket!)

Next we discover that our Lord commanded us to "bear fruit" (John 15:16). Fruit? Isn't that the stuff that starts with a seed and has a slow-growing tree in between?

Then come His instructions to "grow up into him who is the Head" (Ephesians 4:15). Growing up is the slowest thing that happens to a child . . . even slower than waiting for Christmas. And eagerness adds neither an inch to the stature nor a year to the calendar.

Growth isn't fast, yet it does yield high gains. Our Lord explains that "the testing of your faith develops perseverance. Perseverance must finish its work so that you may be mature and complete, not lacking anything" (James 1:3–4).

Still, it might help our patience and perseverance to realize that while there are no instant formulas, God has the most glorious "instant" of all prepared for His children . . .

Listen, I tell you a mystery: We will not all sleep, but we will all be changed—in a flash, in the twinkling of an eye, at the last trumpet. For the trumpet will sound, the dead will be raised imperishable, and we will be changed.

When the perishable has been clothed with the imperishable, and the mortal with immortality, then the saying that is written will come true: "Death has been swallowed up in victory."

But thanks be to God! He gives us the victory through our Lord Jesus Christ. Therefore, my dear brothers (and sisters), stand firm. Let nothing move you. Always give yourselves fully to the work of the Lord, because you know that your labor in the Lord is not in vain.

—1 Corinthians 15:51–52, 54, 57–58

Letter to a Friend

It's our job to introduce our circumstances and feelings to God's resurrection truth.

My *Dear Friend*,

I had such a wonderful time with you the other afternoon, but my heart has been so heavy with your situation and concerns since we talked. I keep praying that God will keep you balanced. You are dealing with so much stress from so many different areas!

It's ironic that I'm in the midst of writing a book about growing through life's storms. When I think of how you're struggling, I am cautioned not to toss out a simplistic challenge to people I've never even met to "trust and *grow* through it all!" (I already felt cautious, but even more so now!)

I know it's not *easy* to trust and look for growth when nothing makes sense—when you're about to lose everything—when there's no peace anywhere—when you feel as if you're the only one in the boat who's rowing. It's all too easy to feel abandoned by an all-powerful, limitless Lord who doesn't appear to be using His power and riches to help when you're clearly going down for the count!

I can't give you (or anyone else) platitudes or easy answers. Because there *are no* easy answers. But I can hold on in faith for you . . . faith in a God of love who won't let us go no matter how bad it looks or feels . . . faith in the work He's doing in you and through you, His beloved child, my dear sister.

And if it does get worse—if God allows you to lose even more that is precious to you—you can be certain that I won't understand or like it any better than you do. I'll probably ask God if He's *sure* this is necessary. I'll probably tell Him you didn't *need* that. I might even get into the subject of what's "fair" and "not fair," like my kids used to do. Because I know that you're doing everything you can possibly do!

But then I'll have to wipe my eyes and go on trusting Him with you. And I'll need to begin praising Him for that hard-to-imagine good that He's *covenanted* to work out for you. Because while *I* don't want to see you *hurting*, I know that *He* won't allow you to be truly *harmed*—even when it hurts and feels like the bottom has dropped out.

May I share one thing with you? When I was carrying you in my heart (everywhere I went the other morning!) I happened to be reading Ray Stedman's book *God's Loving Word*. He was discussing John 19:41–42, which tells us about Joseph of Arimathea and Nicodemus laying Jesus' body in a new tomb in a garden near the place where He was crucified.

Ray writes:

There, in that beautiful garden, just a few yards from the site of Jesus' agony, was this tomb. The cross represented failure and despair.

Certainly, that was the mood of all those who had followed Jesus throughout His earthly ministry, only to see all their hopes nailed to a Roman cross.

But, though Jesus' friends and followers didn't know it then, the place of resurrection was just a few yards from the place of despair and hopelessness. And so it is with you and me.

Perhaps you are feeling a complete bankruptcy of spirit as you read these words. Perhaps you are in a situation which leaves you feeling hopeless. Perhaps, you have been "crucified," unjustly treated by the world around you. Your spirit may be broken, and you see no future ahead of you.

Let me assure you of this: There is a resurrection in your future. You can't see it now, but it is not far away. The empty tomb is near the cross. When you stand close to the cross of Jesus, when you choose to follow the will of God wherever it leads, the Day of Resurrection is just around the corner!

I wait with you, my precious friend. And I hurt and wonder with you. But I also know (as I'm sure some part of you does too) that God has a great "gettin' up mornin'" around the corner for you and your precious family. That corner just won't come soon enough for either one of us!

I love you, I believe in you, and I'll ride this out with you.

Susan

It is right for me to feel this way about . . . you, since I have you in my heart.
—Philippians 1:7

May our Lord Jesus Christ himself and God our Father, who loved us and by his grace gave us eternal encouragement and good hope, encourage your heart and strengthen you in every good deed and word.
But the Lord is faithful, and he will strengthen and protect you from the evil one. May God direct your heart into God's love and Christ's perseverance.
—2 Thessalonians 2:16–17; 3:3, 5

What a Life

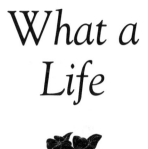

My grandfather always said that living is like licking honey off a thorn.
—Louis Adamic

Life is sweet. It offers sunrises, fat baby fists, darting hummingbirds, commitments, outstretched arms, spring breezes, puppies, giggles, surprise parties, strawberries, voices in harmony, dimples, sheets on a clothesline, curls on little girls, compliments, fresh-baked bread, red wagons, great oak trees, whiskered men, love letters, pink parasols, marching bands, harvest time, feather pillows, waterfalls, boys on bikes, praise songs, full moons, cozy fires, communion, reunion, daisies, helping hands, pounding surf, butterflies, and white clouds mounded in blue skies.

Life is sharp. It pierces with good-byes, fevered brows, screams, empty beds, tornadoes and earthquakes, prejudice, poison ivy, traffic jams, tear-stained cheeks, ignorance, failure, war, drought, explosions, greed, lies, criticism, head-on collisions, rust and rot, floods, doubts, rejection, wrinkles, mosquitoes, hunger, hands that slap or steal, despair, divorce, rape, depression, broken bones, broken promises, broken dreams, broken hearts, broken lives, and dark clouds mounded in gray skies.

How can we enjoy the sweetness of this life without being pricked by its jagged thorns? How can we feel at home in a world blighted by sin yet blessed with the redeeming grace and presence of God?

God's children are not at home here; but we are *here*, nonetheless. And we discover that it's impossible to enjoy this world's sunshine without enduring its clouds and storms. There is no way to withdraw from only one part of life. Resistance to pain inevitably numbs us to joy.

So we accept the reality that this world of clashing darkness and light is where we are required to live and mature. Some day all things will be made new in Christ. But for now, our job is to stand firm and grow where we are planted by using all the sunshine and rain that comes our way. Would we come to harvest without either?

Jesus told this parable: "The kingdom of heaven is like a man who sowed good seed in his field. But while everyone was sleeping, his enemy came and sowed weeds among the wheat, and went away. When the wheat sprouted and formed heads, then the weeds also appeared.

"The owner's servants came to him and said, 'Sir, didn't you sow good seed in your field? Where then did the weeds come from?'

"'An enemy did this,' he replied. The servants asked him, 'Do you want us to go and pull them up?'

"'No,' he answered, 'because while you are pulling the weeds, you may root up the wheat with them. Let both grow together until the harvest. At that time I will tell the harvesters: First collect the weeds and tie them in bundles to be burned; then gather the wheat and bring it into my barn.'"

—Matthew 13:24–30

Weathering
the Storm

**Be still before the LORD and wait patiently for
him.**

—Psalm 37:7

Oh Lord,
let this trouble,
this trial,
cause me to
be still
and know that you are
God.
Use this tension as
surface tension to
hold me,
clinging like a droplet
after a storm,
patiently suspended,

yet holding fast to my
Vine of Life.

The storm swirled, throbbing about my little car as it headed toward the dark mountains. As nature staged the hidden tempest in my soul, my hand moved in rhythm with the windshield wipers doggedly slashing at sliding drops.

Lightning and heartbreak stabbed in jagged flashes. Thunder roared. Leaves and questions tossed wet in the wind.

The torrent poured on before me, yet the sun began to touch and warm my back. A rainbow, soft and wide, embraced the darkest mountain top. "See, I am with you always. I promise, my child. I promise!"

So beautifully God paints understanding and peace with strokes from His own rich palette of promises.

I waited patiently for the LORD; he turned to me and heard my cry. . . . God is our refuge and strength, an ever present help in trouble. Therefore we will not fear, though the earth give way and the mountains fall into the heart of the sea, though its waters roar and foam and the mountains quake with their surging.
—Psalm 40:1; 46:1–3

Where can I go from your Spirit? Where can I flee from your presence? If I go up to the heavens, you are there; if

— 155 —

I make my bed in the depths, you are there. If I rise on the wings of the dawn, if I settle on the far side of the sea, even there your hand will guide me, your right hand will hold me fast. If I say, "Surely the darkness will hide me and the light become night around me, even the darkness will not be dark to you; the night will shine like the day, for darkness is as light to you."

—Psalm 139:7–12

Seeing Beneath and Beyond

You are looking only on the surface of things.
—2 Corinthians 10:7

Looking at the surface of life's present circumstances I can come to several conclusions, all of them factual, all of them miserable.

First, I'm being rained on. Again.

Second, I'm soaking wet and shivering in the winds of adversity. Again.

Third, if "wet is wonderful," then I'm more than wonderful because I'm completely and totally *drenched*.

Menacing storms like this one have been lined up on the horizon of my life like a fleet of planes in a relentless landing pattern.

And I can see absolutely no spiritual progress, no purpose, no good, no gain. From where I stand in the clouds and pouring rain, it's impossible to see what God is doing beneath the surface and beyond the moment.

It *is* possible, however, to *know* without seeing.

Because I know my Heavenly Father. I know He's able to do anything, anywhere, in any weather condition, visibly or invisibly. And whatever He does will always turn out to be good, because *He* is good.

Without seeing, I know that these rains of adversity will soak deep into the soil of who I am and that through it all God will cause me to "take root below and bear fruit above" (2 Kings 19:30). And because of that Root, I will be "filled with the fruit of righteousness that comes through Jesus Christ—to the glory and praise of God" (Philippians 1:11).

God didn't say I should pretend to enjoy this tear-saturated and uncertain landscape. He did say that with eyes of faith I could see *beneath* it to His work within me, and *beyond* it "to the joy set before" me (Hebrews 12:2). . . to the joy set before *us*. He promised His eternal hope for tomorrow, and the grace and peace of His Presence for today.

I'm not alone out in the rain. And neither are you.

We don't yet see things clearly. We're squinting in a fog, peering through a mist. But it won't be long before the weather clears and the sun shines bright! We'll see it all then, see it all as clearly as God sees us, knowing him directly just as he knows us!

—1 Corinthians 13:12, The Message

Now faith is being sure of what we hope for and certain of what we do not see.

Let us fix our eyes on Jesus, the author and perfecter of our faith, who for the joy set before him endured the cross, scorning its shame, and sat down at the right hand of the throne of God. Consider him who endured such opposition from sinful men, so that you will not grow weary and lose heart.

Endure hardship as discipline; God is treating you as sons. For what son is not disciplined by his father? If you are not disciplined (and everyone undergoes discipline), then you are illegitimate children and not true sons. Moreover, we have all had human fathers who disciplined us and we respected them for it. How much more should we submit to the Father of our spirits and live! Our fathers disciplined us for a little while as they thought best; but God disciplines us for our good that we may share in his holiness. No discipline seems pleasant at the time, but painful. Later on, however, it produces a harvest of righteousness and peace for those who have been trained by it.

—Hebrews 11:1; 12:2–3, 7–11

A Rich Inheritance

A good man leaves an inheritance for his children's children.

—Proverbs 13:22

I *can still barely* believe it, but my Dad is gone. When the emergency room nurse took us to the cubicle where he lay, his arm had slipped and was dangling over the edge of the narrow bed. Instinctively, I reached for his hand. It was cold. Already. Those strong, wonderful hands that were always fixing or building something to help someone, could no longer squeeze back in loving response.

Tears sprang to my eyes as I stood with my sister, brother, and husband, transfixed by the sweeping movement of the second hand on Dad's wristwatch. Strange that his timepiece should continue to measure the passing minutes when he had just entered a timeless eternity with the Lord. My brother gently slid the watch from his wrist. Time only counted for us.

I took one last good-bye look at his face—ashen now—that used to crinkle into warmth so often. The long sutured welt across the top of his head seemed intrusive—an unnecessary wounding. He was truly gone from his body. And I was truly not ready for this.

When I had left for my speaking trip to Great Britain he was, to all appearances, his usual independent, healthy self. How could a brain tumor have taken him so quickly? When I phoned home (only four days after my previous call) he had already been through surgery and the dreadful diagnosis had been pronounced. Highly malignant. Fast-growing. Terminal. They said he would lose his mind and be totally paralyzed before it was over. Oh, God, please, not like that!

Against great odds my husband and I got an early flight home and I had three precious visits with Dad. Then, mercifully, instantaneously, God took him home. A massive hemorrhage from the site of the tumor. One minute he was sitting in a wheelchair struggling to brush his teeth with the hand that still worked; the next minute he was standing face to face with his wonderful Savior. And he surely stood arm in arm with his beloved wife of more than fifty years, my mother.

The whole thing—diagnosis, surgery, paralysis, prayers for help, and this final answer to prayer—took less than a month from start to finish.

So we buried his body and celebrated his home-going at a memorial service filled with crying, remembering, rejoicing, holding one another close, and holding one another up.

And now, because I'm committed to writing this book about the blessings God seeks to bring to us through life's storms, I'm trying to figure out what possible gain there could be in such an unexpected, heartrending tornado of loss as this has been . . . a loss I felt, and continue to feel, deeply.

Certainly I knew that my parents could not always be here—that someday they would die, just as we all will. But the fact is, from my earliest memories Dad always *has* been here. He was the one who taught me to know and love God. He was the rock, the steady, faithful God-honoring head of our family. And he *prayed* for me. Daily, my earthly father had a talk with his Heavenly Father about their daughter. How would I make it without those prayers?

And in the last few years—especially since Mom's death—I had grown used to Dad showing up at our front door with a big bear hug or two and a hankering for some home cooking—a thick slice or two of my honey oatmeal bread accompanied by a steaming bowl of chili, or my slow-simmered pot roast with mashed potatoes and gravy, especially when it was followed by a big wedge of fresh green apple pie, or strawberry shortcake (if the berries were good and sweet). When he came he enjoyed my food, my well-stocked bookshelves, and my company—not necessarily in that order. How would I make it without him and his loving hugs? Where are the *gains* in all these losses?

Could I have gained *appreciation?* Certainly loss deepened it. My father was a good man who had always made me feel secure and loved without saying a word. In his later years, to my great delight, he learned to openly express his affection and to hear and receive my love and appreciation. I'm confident that God is telling him now how very grateful I am for the wonderful, prayerful father He gave me. I'm counting on God to bless him with glories and joys beyond my imagination. So at least Dad has gained a fuller appreciation of my appreciation! (But since heaven is such a happy place, I suspect God won't mention how much I'm missing him.)

Could I also have gained *wisdom and perspective?* I hope so. Psalm 90:12 says, "Teach us to number our days aright, that we may gain a heart of wisdom." Sudden loss reminds us to measure our days, and our struggles, against the backdrop of eternity, for our time on earth is very short. Wisdom encourages us to:

Say love that's unsaid. Now.

Let go of what might keep us apart. Now.

Give while there's a hand to receive. Now.

Hug, laugh, cry, sing, and share our hearts. Now.

For what we dare to give to one another in love enriches us at the time, stays behind to comfort and help at our parting, yet still goes on to heaven—a seed to flower in eternity, bringing perennial joy.

But my biggest gain in this storm of loss is surely my *rich inheritance*. When I spoke at the memorial service I said, "Dad was never wealthy in this world's ways, so I'm not expecting much of an inheritance in material things from him. In fact, I feel that I've already received my inheritance from Dad."

My brothers and sisters and I do have a valuable inheritance. We were born to a father rich in faith and courage. He remained steadfast, and he prayed, loved, believed, and lived out his hope in Christ. We have inherited an example of faithfulness that can never be taken away. And because Dad "worked at it with all his heart, as working for the Lord, not for men," I know that he "will receive an inheritance from the Lord as a reward" (Colossians 3:23–24.)

We who follow his example will receive the same reward, for our Heavenly Father waits with an unperishable inheritance for those of us who continue to walk in faith and prayer, believing.

Praise be to the God and Father of our Lord Jesus Christ! In his great mercy he has given us new birth into a living hope through the resurrection of Jesus Christ from the dead, and into an inheritance that can never perish, spoil or fade—kept in heaven for you, who through faith are shielded by God's power until the coming of the salvation that is ready to be revealed in the last time. In this you greatly rejoice, though now for a little while you may have had to suffer grief in all kinds of trials. These have come so that your faith—of greater worth than gold, which perishes even though refined by fire—may be proved genuine and may result in praise, glory and honor when Jesus Christ is revealed. Though you have not seen him, you love him; and even though you do not see him now, you believe in him and are filled with an inexpressible and glorious joy, for you are receiving the goal of your faith, the salvation of your souls.

—1 Peter 1:3–9

Rooted by
the Storm

I'm prone to
huddle in life's storms,
to crouch 'neath winds and rain.
Should faith unfurl
my cringing soul and
stand me tall in Christ—
what then?
"Whose feet are planted firm in Me,
is rooted by the storm."

Others went out on the sea in ships; they were merchants
on the mighty waters. They saw the works of the LORD,
his wonderful deeds in the deep. For he spoke and stirred
up a tempest that lifted high the waves. They mounted up
to the heavens and went down to the depths; in their peril
their courage melted away. They reeled and staggered
like drunken men; they were at their wits' end. Then they

cried out to the LORD in their trouble, and he brought them out of their distress. He stilled the storm to a whisper; the waves of the sea were hushed.

—Psalm 107:23–29

One day he and his disciples got in a boat. "Let's cross the lake," he said. And off they went. It was smooth sailing, and he fell asleep. A terrific storm came up suddenly on the lake. Water poured in, and they were about to capsize. They woke Jesus: "Master, Master, we're going to drown!"

Getting to his feet, he told the wind, "Silence!" and the waves, "Quiet down!" They did it. The lake became smooth as glass.

Then he said to his disciples, "Why can't you trust me?"

They were in absolute awe, staggered and stammering, "Who is this, anyway? He calls out to the winds and sea, and they do what he tells them!"

—Luke 8:22–25, The Message

A Lecture
to Myself at
Pruning Season

**There is no way that we can be effective disciples
of Christ except through relentless pruning—the
cutting away of non-fruitbearing suckers that sap
our energies, but bear no fruit.**

—Selwyn Hughes, *The Divine Gardener*

Look at you. What a restless branch you are—squirming, aching, offering suggestions, and protesting in
the hands of your Lord.

Stop fighting! Stop trying so hard to understand
it all, to make the changes, to know the direction
and outcome of this pruning.

Rest. Just rest and remain in Him. You know He
can be trusted. So trust.

Trust enough to stop trying to be His special assistant. He doesn't need the help. Trust enough to let yourself cry for what is and what isn't. Trust enough to praise and thank your Vine for what is and what will be.

Trust enough to take a nap, for goodness' sake!

"I am the true vine and my Father is the gardener. He cuts off every branch in me that bears no fruit, while every branch that does bear fruit he prunes so that it will be even more fruitful. Remain in me, and I will remain in you. No branch can bear fruit by itself; it must remain in the vine. Neither can you bear fruit unless you remain in me."
—John 15:1–2, 4

No discipline seems pleasant at the time, but painful. Later on, however, it produces a harvest of righteousness and peace for those who have been trained by it.
—Hebrews 12:11

Climbing Through Life's Clutter

If you falter in times of trouble, how small is your strength.

—Proverbs 24:10

It's hard to miss those
boulders of trouble that
roll into my life.
They're big enough
to climb on so I
take Your hand, Jesus,
and scramble up with Your help.
It's those pebbles of
pressure,
noise,
and everyday frustration

that are nearly stoning
me senseless.
Lord, toughen my hide and
soften my heart.
Teach me to walk that slow,
winding cobblestone path to
Christian maturity.

So do not throw away your confidence; it will be richly rewarded. You need to persevere so that when you have
done the will of God, you will receive what he has promised. For in just a very little while, "He who is coming will
come and will not delay. But my righteous one will live by
faith. And if he shrinks back, I will not be pleased with
him." But we are not of those who shrink back and are
destroyed, but of those who believe and are saved.
—Hebrews 10:35–39

Poem reprinted from *When the Handwriting on the Wall Is in
Brown Crayon,* © 1981 Susan L. Lenzkes.

When Evil Rains Down

"Whoever serves me must follow me; and where I am, my servant also will be."
—John 12:26

I *watch the evening news and squirm as the*
world's soot settles over me,
the latest dregs of national gossip,
teeming international inequities,
sordid statistics of greed and compromise,
blatant sin paraded as human rights,
the pollution of violence, oppression, misery.
I long to escape the debris of this broken world that
sifts down
spoiling serenity
soiling peace and joy.
Yet dare I close my eyes to the pain that my Lord
carried on His back?

He watched the evening news
and staggered to the cross.

For God so loved the world that he gave his one and only Son, that whoever believes in him shall not perish but have eternal life. For God did not send his Son into the world to condemn the world, but to save the world through him.

—John 3:16–17

You see, at just the right time, when we were still powerless, Christ died for the ungodly. Very rarely will anyone die for a righteous man, though for a good man someone might possibly dare to die. But God demonstrates his own love for us in this: While we were still sinners, Christ died for us.

For if, when we were God's enemies, we were reconciled to him through the death of his Son, how much more, having been reconciled, shall we be saved through his life!

—Romans 5:6–8, 10

I tell you, open your eyes and look at the fields! They are ripe for harvest . . . even now he harvests the crop for eternal life . . .

—John 4:35–36

He said to them, "Go into all the world and preach [this] good news to all creation."

—Mark 16:15

Let us not become weary in doing good, for at the proper time we will reap a harvest if we do not give up.

—Galatians 6:9

To Name a Fear

Who is more foolish, the child afraid of the dark,
or the man afraid of the light?
—Maurice Freehill

The subject of my Tuesday morning women's Bible
study class was fear, and it was with a certain amount
of fear that I went off to teach it because I knew I
would have to begin with a confession.

While preparing the lesson that week, I had rev-
eled in the satisfaction that I'm not a fearful person.
I've never had to wrestle with the vicious lions of
fear that I've seen roar through some people's lives
and tear them apart.

Just about then the Lord poked His finger
through the veneer of my smug attitude, pointing out
the sleeping cat that I call Tabby. Instead of dealing
with my fear, I made a pet out of it. Instead of con-

quering it, I patted it on the head and fed it saucers of milk!

How dangerous fear is when it purrs rather than roars. For when we don't recognize it as an enemy we allow it to curl up and stay on the hearth of our lives.

And while claiming that we're not "afraid," we are nevertheless concerned, worried, restless, anxious, bored, frequently sick, and unmotivated (or else working frantically). Or we feel guilty, indecisive, possessive, defensive, negative, shy, or tired—oh, so tired!

It takes a brave person to admit, "I'm worried because I'm afraid you'll . . ." "I can't choose because I fear that if . . ." "I'm so tired from working hard to prevent . . ." "I feel vulnerable when . . ." "But what if . . ."

The masks of fear are many and varied. They need to be uncovered and exposed to the Light of the World, Who says, "Fear not!" For He knows how many things in this world evoke fear in His children.

When we're ready to call our fear by its first name, we're ready to receive Jesus' antidote to fear—which is simply (or sometimes not so simply) the faith to trust in Him. He is able.

Then he placed his right hand on me and said: "Do not be afraid. I am the Living One; I was dead, and behold I am alive for ever and ever!"
—Revelation 1:17–18

The LORD is my light and my salvation—whom shall I fear? The LORD is the stronghold of my life—of whom shall I be afraid? When evil men advance against me to devour my flesh, when my enemies and my foes attack me, they will stumble and fall. Though an army besiege me, even then will I be confident. For in the day of trouble he will keep me safe in his dwelling; he will hide me in the shelter of his tabernacle and set me high upon a rock.

—Psalm 27:1–3, 5

I sought the LORD, and he answered me; he delivered me from all my fears. Those who look to him are radiant; their faces are never covered with shame.

—Psalm 34:4–5

Daily
Sprinkles

I want to grow, Lord.
It's all right with me
if You send some trial my way
so I'll learn to lean on Your strength.
Don't spare me by making it small—
send a big biblical blast of
holy refining fire.
Don't let my bickering children,
this tension headache,
the incessantly ringing telephone,
these broken dishes,
this draining tiredness,
the heat and smog
or these boring repetitive tasks
distract me—
so that when a trial comes
I miss it.

It would be such a shame
if I overlooked my chance
to grow closer to You!

You let the distress bring you to God, not drive you from him. The result was all gain, no loss.

Distress that drives us to God does that. It turns us around. It gets us back in the way of salvation. We never regret that kind of pain. But those who let distress drive them away from God are full of regrets, end up on a deathbed of regrets.

And now, isn't it wonderful all the ways in which this distress has goaded you closer to God? You're more alive, more concerned, more sensitive, more reverent, more human, more passionate, more responsible. Looked at from any angle, you've come out of this with purity of heart.

—2 Corinthians 7:9–11, The Message

I'm Not Good Enough

One does not sow and reap in the same day.
—John Claypool

One of life's biggest discouragements is the disparity between the high plain for which my soul cries out and the valley where I generally plow my crooked furrows. Over the years I have often brought to the Lord my need to do better than I do and be better than I am.

There is nothing wrong with stretching for the best, with reaching toward the perfection that will one day be our inheritance. Even the apostle Paul must have felt this way for he said, "Not that I have already obtained all this, or have already been made perfect, but I press on to take hold of that for which Christ Jesus took hold of me" (Philippians 3:12).

The trouble begins not when I obediently and faithfully press on toward the goal of being made perfect in Christ; it begins when I am a perfectionist. A perfectionist resists the truth that growing up in Christ is a process. After all, we read the Bible and we know what He intends us to be. So we should be that way now. Such thinking creates its own storms and difficulties.

We struggle so hard to achieve perfection that we become exhausted and joyless. We fail to own or appreciate our humanity, even though God has declared His chosen dwelling place to be with us, just as we are.

All this creates an even bigger problem. As perfectionists we find it difficult, if not impossible, to believe that God could completely accept, love, and long to be with us in this unfinished state. We speak of His love and freedom, but we don't rest in it.

We allowed God's grace to save us, but somehow it doesn't seem enough to keep us (though we would never actually say that). We say "God's grace is sufficient for us" but we act as if grace is given to strengthen our efforts to earn His love. Such deeply imbedded attitudes isolate us in a prison of endless striving and eventual despair.

Peace comes only when we acknowledge that human effort cannot sustain righteousness any more than it could create it. God's truth waits to set us free as we acknowledge that our most disciplined effort can create only an image, a mere picture, of righteousness. And we all know that even the most beautiful picture of a tree can produce no real fruit.

Our Heavenly Gardener waits for access to the earthy loam of our life and heart—as we are today. Only then can He begin to plow, plant, and nourish His seeds of true and lasting righteousness.

Let me put this question to you: how did your new life begin? Was it by working your heads off to please God? Or was it by responding to God's Message to you? Are you going to continue this craziness? For only crazy people would think they could complete by their own efforts what was begun by God. If you weren't smart enough or strong enough to begin it, how do you suppose you could perfect it? Did you go through this whole painful learning process for nothing?

—Galatians 3:3–4, The Message

The former regulation is set aside because it was weak and useless (for the law made nothing perfect), and a better hope is introduced, by which we draw near to God. Therefore [Jesus Christ] is able to save completely those who come to God through him, because he always lives to intercede for them. Such a high priest meets our need—one who is holy, blameless, pure, set apart from sinners, exalted above the heavens. Because by one sacrifice he has made perfect forever those who are being made holy.

—Hebrews 7:18, 25–26; 10:14

Continue to work out your salvation with fear and trembling, for it is God who works in you to will and to act according to his good purpose.

—Philippians 2:12–13

So neither he who plants nor he who waters is anything, but only God, who makes things grow.

—1 Corinthians 3:7

Cultivating Joy

What has happened to all your joy?
—Galatians 4:15

Through His great and
precious promises,
God generously sprinkles
His seeds of joy in our hearts.
Yet too often we reap a
harvest of misery.
Joy's seed
requires deep furrows of faith,
sprouts in the rich soil of trust,
is nourished by daily
soaking in God's Word,
blossoms in eager response to
His love,
grows strong through

winds of adversity,
and bears fruit only as we
stay rooted in obedience to
Christ's commands.
And how true that
the tender seedling of
God's joy
and the stubborn weed of
self-pity
cannot survive in the same garden!

Joy is not mere happiness. Nor does joy spring from a life of ease, comfort, or peaceful circumstances. Joy is the soul's buoyant response to a God of promise, presence, and power.

Joy lifts our spirit above earth's sorrow, dancing in jubilation at the hope set before us. Joy is faith feasting and celebrating the One in Whom it trusts. Joy is the heart vibrating in grateful rhythm to the love of Almighty God who actually chooses to make His home within us. Joy is the child of God reclining in the luxury of a Father Who is "able to do immeasurably more than all we ask or imagine according to his power that is at work within us" (Ephesians 3:20).

Joy is the vine-ripened fruit grown of God's own Spirit Who is at work within us as we trust and obey—and it is sweet to both God and man.

The fruit of the Spirit is love, joy . . .
—Galatians 5:22

*If you obey my commands, you will remain in my love,
just as I have obeyed my Father's commands and remain
in his love. I have told you this so that my joy may be in
you and that your joy may be complete.*
—John 15:10–11

*As the rain and the snow come down from heaven, and
do not return to it without watering the earth and making
it bud and flourish, so that it yields seed for the sower and
bread for the eater, so is my word that goes out from my
mouth: It will not return to me empty, but will accomplish what I desire and achieve the purpose for which I
sent it. You will go out in joy and be led forth in peace:
the mountains and hills will burst into song before you,
and all the trees of the field will clap their hands.*
—Isaiah 55:10–12

*The desert and the parched land will be glad; the wilder-
ness will rejoice and blossom. Like the crocus, it will
burst into bloom; it will rejoice greatly and shout for joy.
Gladness and joy will overtake them, and sorrow and
sighing will flee away.*
—Isaiah 35:1–2, 10

For the LORD your God will bless you in all your harvest and in all the work of your hands, and your joy will be complete.

—Deuteronomy 16:15

Melting Boredom

A rut is a grave with the ends knocked out.
—Laurence J. Peter

Boredom *was smothering* me in the orange heat of that long ago afternoon when my little boy rushed in with his announcement. "I know how to catch a moth now, Mommy!" To demonstrate he stalked, straddle-legged, across the kitchen floor, elbows flung out, hands perched to pounce. "And then you grab him. Like this!" And he attacked a spot on the floor with his powerful five-year-old pincher grip.

"I see," I said, amused. "That looks pretty good. But moths are hard to catch. They have wings—you don't!"

"I can do it, don't worry."

"Well, what if you do catch one?" I continued, determined to confound this seemingly impossible plan before it disappointed him. "How will you feed it? What do moths like to eat?"

"Oh, flowers, I guess."

So he spent all afternoon filling plastic sandwich bags with one surprised moth and one small yellow marigold each. I spent all afternoon learning that boredom is candle wax beneath the flaming wick of enthusiasm. And I began to understand something else, too.

When we allow ourselves to become bored, when we lose our sense of adventure, we grow *older* but not *wiser*. Wisdom enlarges our capacity for discovery and delight, causing wonder to grow as we grow.

We'll spend eternity exploring and rejoicing in the unsearchable riches of God's character, purpose, love, Living Word, and astounding creativity. We need to begin on this earth. What a joy to catch the wonder of God's work around us, and *in* us!

Open my eyes that I may see wonderful things. . . . I am
a stranger on earth; . . . To all perfection I see a limit;
but your commands are boundless.
　　　　　　　　—Psalm 119:18-19, 96

Great is the LORD and most worthy of praise: his great-
ness no one can fathom. One generation will commend
your works to another; they will tell of your mighty acts.
They will speak of the glorious splendor of your majesty,

and I will meditate on your wonderful works. They will celebrate your abundant goodness and sing of your righteousness.

—Psalm 145:3–5, 7

The secret things belong to the LORD our God, but the things revealed belong to us and to our children forever . . .

—Deuteronomy 29:29

At that time Jesus said, "I praise you, Father, Lord of heaven and earth, because you have hidden these things from the wise and learned, and revealed them to little children. Yes, Father, for this was your good pleasure.

—Matthew 11:25–26

New Beginnings

The best thing about the future is that it comes only one day at a time.

—Abraham Lincoln

The beginning of a new year—always an experience in tentative hope! Those midnight chimes that ring out the old year and bring in the new seem to chant, "What lies ahead?"

And feeling both fear and trust within us, we grope to join hands in fortress against the unknown. Secret dreads chip away the edges of new chances. Precious ties dangle loosely. Clocks tick ever faster.

Yet pushing up through our apprehension like a crocus through snow is the bright delight of opportunity. For there sits that calendar, fresh and yawning to be filled with dreams achieved and goals attained. And there stands our Lord saying, "Fear not, just fol-

low Me. I am the same yesterday, today, and forever"
(see Hebrews 13:8).

*When times are good, be happy; but when times are bad,
consider: God has made the one as well as the other.
Therefore, a man cannot discover anything about his
future.*
—Ecclesiastes 7:14

*"For I know the plans I have for you," declares the
LORD, "plans to prosper you and not to harm you, plans
to give you hope and a future."*
—Jeremiah 29:11

*Since you are my rock and my fortress, for the sake of
your name lead and guide me. . . . I trust in you, O
LORD. I say, "You are my God." My times are in your
hands. . . .*
—Psalm 31:3, 14–15

*Jesus . . . said, "I am the light of the world. Whoever fol-
lows me will never walk in darkness, but will have the
light of life."*
—John 8:12

Trust

Blessed is the man who trusts in the LORD, whose trust is the LORD.
                    —Jeremiah 17:7 RSV

Stoop-shouldered,
foot-dragging,
sighing
resignation
is not trust.
Real trust
bounces on eager toes of
anticipation—
laughs with the pure delight
of knowing
in whom it believes—
rests easy
knowing
on whom it waits.
Lord,
so wrap me in the

knowledge of You
that my trust is no longer
in You, but
is You.

Children are cutest when no one's watching—or they think no one is.

I had just stepped into the kitchen with an armload of laundry when the sight of our boys standing together on the back step caught my eye. Their backs were turned, so they didn't see me looking as the little one wrapped his arm around his brother's knees and tilted his blond head back, gazing up. He barely reached his brother's belt loops.

In a tiny voice he said, "Bend your ear down a minute—I want to tell you a secret."

Then, very quietly, he whispered something that delighted them both.

You know, Jesus, I can't help thinking as I watch them . . . after all these years of walking with You, I still don't even stretch to Your knees. Bend Your ear down a minute, I want to tell You a secret. I think You're wonderful. And I really do trust You. When I grow up I want to be just like You.

Blessed is the man [woman] who makes the LORD *his [her] trust.*

—*Psalm 40:4*

For you have been my hope, O Sovereign LORD, my confidence since my youth. From birth I have relied on you; you brought me forth from my mother's womb. I will ever praise you. Since my youth, O God, you have taught me, and to this day I declare your marvelous deeds. Even when I am old and gray, do not forsake me, O God, till I declare your power to the next generation, your might to all who are to come.

—Psalm 71:5–6, 17–18

I will say of the LORD, "He is my refuge and my fortress, my God, in whom I trust."

—Psalm 91:2

Excerpted from *When the Handwriting on the Wall Is in Brown Crayon*, copyright © 1981 Susan L. Lenzkes.

Five Ways to Handle Fear and Worry

Worry does not empty tomorrow of its sorrow, it empties today of its strength.

—Corrie ten Boom

I *once knew someone so
simple-minded and unaware
that fear never entered her world.
Worry never invaded her innocence.
Ignorance became bliss.*

*I once knew someone so
informed and educated
that future fears stalked her world.
Worry endlessly postulated doom.
Intelligence became dread.*

I once knew someone so
idealistic and spiritual
that fear was denied.
Worry disguised itself as repetitious prayers.
Ideology became escapism.

I once knew someone so
capable and determined
that fear was a challenge to avoid disaster.
Worry simply required more work.
Intervention became exhaustion.

I once knew someone so
realistic and wise
that she feared and trusted only God.
This world's worries were placed in His hands.
Inability became peace.

"And he asked them, 'Why were you so fearful? Don't you even yet have confidence in me?'"
—Jesus Christ, Mark 4:40 LB

"I tell you, my friends, do not be afraid of those who kill the body and after that can do no more. But I will show you whom you should fear: Fear him who, after the killing of the body, has the power to throw you into hell. Yes, I tell you, fear him. Are not five sparrows sold for two pennies? Yet not one of them is forgotten by God. Indeed, the very hairs of your head are all numbered. Don't be afraid; you are worth more than many sparrows."
—Luke 12:4–7

There is no fear in love. But perfect love drives out fear, because fear has to do with punishment. The one who fears is not made perfect in love. We love because he first loved us.

—1 John 4:18–19

Cast all your anxiety on him because he cares for you.

—1 Peter 5:7

God has said, "Never will I leave you; never will I forsake you." So we say with confidence, "The Lord is my helper; I will not be afraid. What can man do to me?"

—Hebrews 13:5–6

Walking While Waiting

With your help I can advance . . .
—2 Samuel 22:30

Sometimes we are certain that we're going nowhere in life. We are trapped between the walls of some narrow, spartan place that we're sure must be one of life's dreary waiting rooms. So we sit down, reach for an outdated periodical, and wait for someone to open a door and call our name.

Many of us who think we are being patient may actually be camping out in one of life's hallways! Our Lord's house has many rooms, and how can we get from one to another except through a hallway? Yes, some are long, some narrow, some dark, and some cold. Yet if we fail to understand the purpose of a hallway, we're likely to wander about for years, assuming we are "waiting on the Lord."

Life's hallways *are* places of transition even though we see no change. And because God is with us, such places offer our finest progress.

When faith holds out a hand to God in the dark, we're already *there* even though we haven't yet *arrived*. Waiting on God is the same as walking with God toward exciting new rooms of potential and service.

But we can't see progress in a dark hallway. And although we don't like being stuck there without a flashlight, few other places are so quiet and devoid of outside distractions.

Windowless halls can be the perfect place to discover God and His quiet grace. They are places where time seems to stand still and so we stop and give names to our deepest needs and then give them up to God's care and timing.

On days when we're feeling tired or hopelessly lost, He carries us in His arms. At other times He waits until we grope for His hand and begin to follow along, learning to walk by *faith*, not by *sight*.

When we finally arrive at the door that swings open into the light, we realize that our Heavenly Father can see perfectly well in the dark. We can trust Him to bring us to the next door in His perfect time—the time that will most benefit us and the glory of His name.

Let's practice waiting on the Lord even as we faithfully walk the narrow way.

Let your eyes look straight ahead, fix your gaze directly before you. Make level paths for your feet and take only ways that are firm. Do not swerve to the right or the left; keep your foot from evil.
—Proverbs 4:25–27

But one thing I do: Forgetting what is behind and straining toward what is ahead, I press on toward the goal to win the prize for which God has called me heavenward in Christ Jesus. All of us who are mature should take such a view of things.
—Philippians 3:14–15

Rejoice in the Lord always. I will say it again: Rejoice! Let your gentleness be evident to all. The Lord is near. Do not be anxious about anything, but in everything, by prayer and petition, with thanksgiving, present your requests to God. And the peace of God, which transcends all understanding, will guard your hearts and your minds in Christ Jesus. For I have learned to be content whatever the circumstances. I can do everything through him who gives me strength.
—Philippians 4:4–7, 11, 13

You are my lamp, O LORD; the LORD turns my darkness into light. It is God who arms me with strength and makes

my way perfect. You broaden the path beneath me, so that my ankles do not turn.
—2 Samuel 22:29, 33, 37

God's Exchange System

To all who mourn . . . he will give: Beauty for ashes; Joy instead of mourning; Praise instead of heaviness.

—Isaiah 61:3 LB

Whenever we bow in real understanding before our Lord—whether it's at the cradle, the cross, or the empty tomb; whether we're seeing Him as Savior, Friend, or conquering King—we will long to give Him some wonderful, worthy gift. The Eastern Wise Men brought gold, frankincense, and myrrh!

But we know how it is, how it has always been. We come to Him dressed in the rags of sin—and He gives us His robe of righteousness. We offer our empty, broken hearts—and He fills them with healing love.

We bring Him needs—He supplies His endless resources. We give tears—He gives comfort. We give weakness—He gives grace. We cry out our fears and questions—He whispers His peace and purpose. We present ignorance wrapped in pride—He returns wisdom wrapped in humility.

He knows how it is, how it has always been, and yet He pleads with us to continue to come to Him and give all that we are and all that we are not.

Because He knows something else. He knows that when we have finally given Him all that we are and have received all that He is, we will at last hold the One Gift worth giving away.

Our gold is surrender; our frankincense, praise; our myrrh, loving obedience to His command to give as generously as He has given unto us. He receives such gifts with joy.

Does the LORD delight in burnt offerings and sacrifices as much as in obeying the voice of the LORD? To obey is better than sacrifice, and to heed than the fat of rams.
—1 Samuel 15:22

Through Jesus, therefore, let us continually offer to God a sacrifice of praise—the fruit of lips that confess his name. And do not forget to do good and to share with others, for with such sacrifices God is pleased.
—Hebrews 13:15–16

We know that we have come to know him if we obey his commands. If anyone obeys his word, God's love is truly made complete in him. This is how we know we are in him: Whoever claims to live in him must walk as Jesus did.

—1 John 2:3, 5–6

"Give, and it will be given to you. A good measure, pressed down, shaken together and running over, will be poured into your lap. For with the measure you use, it will be measured to you."

—Luke 6:38

I have neither silver nor gold, but I will give you what I have.

—Acts 3:6 MLB

Free from Misconceptions

**Stand fast therefore in the liberty by which Christ
has made us free, and do not be entangled again . . .**
—Galatians 5:1 NKJV

W*hat daily doings—*
and undoings—
loosen the laces of
our shiny Sunday shoes of
certainty about God and His ways?
We learned to tie them—
so proud—
practicing carefully,
seeking smiles.
But when life's riddles and pain begin to
work loose those
securely tugged knots that assured us
of an easy, predictable life with God,

when we trip on our

    trailing laces

    and sit looking at their

    frayed and soiled ends;

when we can't keep things

    all tied up anymore,

dare we step out of our familiar

    shiny "pat answers" to

    walk on in Truth's barefoot freedom?

For our God is neither

    simple nor manageable,

but He is

    loving and trustworthy.

Your righteousness reaches to the skies, O God, you who have done great things. Who, O God, is like you? Though you have made me see troubles, many and bitter, you will restore my life again; from the depths of the earth you will again bring me up. You will increase my honor and comfort me once again. I will praise you with the harp for your faithfulness, O my God; I will sing praise to you with the lyre, O Holy One of Israel. My lips will shout for joy when I sing praise to you—I, whom you have redeemed.

                      —Psalm 71:19–23

Who's Hurting Now?

Jesus,
I'll know who's
    number one
    if I count the
    tears.
Have I shed more
    for your grief,
    or mine?

When life is difficult, we might try setting aside our own pain and ask God what hurts Him. Does it hurt Him when He shows us the beauty of His light and we turn away toward darkness? When He fits us with the spectacles of His heavenly view and we grope myopically? When He offers uncommon guidance and we follow our own common sense? When He shows us *the* Way and we are content to take *any old* way?

Do His eyes get misty when He spreads a banquet of love before us and we pass it up to nibble on the dry crumbs of hate and resentment? When He offers power to move mountains and we stumble over dirt clods? When He delivers us from evil and we wink at His Enemy? When we cling to Him in pain and then wave to Him in ease? When He presents peace and we battle over it? When He offers salvation to all and we hoard it as a private joy? When we cry out to Him to save us but refuse to live in the safety of His presence?

He waits to help in our weakness, sin, and failure. He already shared *our* pain. When we begin to understand *His* pain, growth begins.

> *"For my thoughts are not your thoughts, neither are your ways my ways," declares the* LORD. *"As the heavens are higher than the earth, so are my ways higher than your ways and my thoughts than your thoughts."*
> —Isaiah 55:8–9

> *God looks down from heaven on the sons [and daughters] of men to see if there are any who understand, any who seek God. Will the evildoers never learn—those who . . . do not call on God? There they were, overwhelmed with dread, where there was nothing to dread.*
> —Psalm 53:2, 4–5

Teach me your way, O LORD, and I will walk in your truth; give me an undivided heart that I may fear your name. I will praise you, O LORD my God, with all my heart; I will glorify your name forever. For great is your love toward me.

—Psalm 86:11–13

I will instruct you and teach you in the way you should go; I will counsel you and watch over you. Do not be like the horse or the mule, which have no understanding but must be controlled by bit and bridle or they will not come to you. Many are the woes of the wicked, but the LORD's unfailing love surrounds the man [woman] who trusts in him. Rejoice in the LORD and be glad, you righteous; sing, all you who are upright in heart!

—Psalm 32:8–11

"Your fruitfulness comes from me." Who is wise? He will realize these things. Who is discerning? He will understand them. The ways of the LORD are right; and the righteous walk in them, but the rebellious stumble in them.

—Hosea 14:8–9

Perspectives
on Pain

What do people mean when they say, "I am not afraid of God because I know He is good"? Have they never even been to a dentist?

—C. S. Lewis

C. S. Lewis had a great mind and a great faith, both of which were shaped on the anvil of living and loving in this broken world. He was a realist. And he was honest. He permitted the questions that pain brings. I suspect he had learned that faith speaks loudest to fears that are faced.

When he and his beloved wife, Joy, were dealing with her terminal illness, he commented to a friend in a letter, "We are not necessarily doubting that God will do the best for us; we are wondering how painful the best will turn out to be."

My husband and I are wondering the same thing. Recently Herb was told his cancer is active again—the doctor mentioned it only a few days before his body began to spread the painful news. He has now begun treatment with an experimental drug that we pray God will use to bring him back into remission—a rarity at this stage of his illness. So we don't really know what God has ahead for us. We are living by faith in a hailstorm of uncertainty.

Our visibility is hampered in these weather conditions. It's easy to see misery and need—they are right in front of our eyes. Pain medications are increasing, and Herb is moving with greater difficulty. But to see through this storm to a future and a hope is more difficult. Through tears, we strain to see God's goodness and purpose.

How thankful we are that, long before these dark clouds gathered, the apostle Paul prayed for our vision problem. His words are recorded in Ephesians 1:18–19: "I pray also that the eyes of your heart may be enlightened in order that you may know the hope to which he has called you, the riches of his glorious inheritance in the saints, and his incomparably great power for us who believe."

A light to cut through the darkness of this earth's storms? Eyes to see hope in a seemingly hopeless situation? A rich inheritance that's not way out there somewhere, lost in the dark? And God's great power, right here, right now, waiting to act on my behalf, waiting to be believed?

So "hope," and the "riches of Christ," and the "power of God" come as we are huddled in our corner of heartache. And we are comforted, yes, but we also gain perspective. Such perspective keeps us from blaming God for bringing this trouble to us. It keeps us from focusing on our fear of the pain. Instead it allows us to begin to praise Him for using this trouble for our good and His glory, even if we never see it on this earth. It helps us to trust His purpose in the midst.

All of this is true, and it sounds so good in the daylight when I'm writing about the realities of life as a child of God. But at midnight—and it's midnight now—it hurts to believe the truth. I want to call up a friend and say, "Can any of this actually be right? It just doesn't seem fair! This dear man who has been my strength shouldn't have to be suffering; he shouldn't be struggling to stand, or jerking in his sleep like this. Can this frightening disease actually be allowed in God's plan? And is God with us now in this room, surrounding and caring for us as I cry while my husband sleeps fitfully?"

Yes, He's here now.

And I find a certainty gripping me—a deep knowledge: God doesn't waste anything. Not doubts or rain; not suffering or pain.

From the suffering of His Son, He produced salvation. He leaves it to us to prove what He will create if we trust Him through our pain.

*In our hearts we felt the sentence of death. But this hap-
pened that we might not rely on ourselves but on God,
who raises the dead. He has delivered us from such a
deadly peril, and he will deliver us. On him we have set
our hope that he will continue to deliver us, as you help
us by your prayers. Then many will give thanks on our
behalf for the gracious favor granted us in answer to the
prayers of many. . . . Now it is God who makes both us
and you stand firm in Christ. He anointed us, set his seal
of ownership on us, and put his Spirit in our hearts as a
deposit guaranteeing what is to come.*
   —2 Corinthians 1:9–11, 21–22

*I consider that our present sufferings are not worth com-
paring with the glory that will be revealed in us.*
   —Romans 8:18

He Still Lights the Darkness

The people living in darkness have seen a great light; . . . on those living in the land of the shadow of death a light has dawned.
—Isaiah 9:2, Matthew 4:16

*What was December twenty-fifth
before it was Christmas?
Just a chilly day
twenty-five sighs into an
endless winter night.
But when it became Christmas—
oh, when it became Christmas
it glowed!*

A *star, radiant and* compelling, announced Christ's birth. Yet it could not have been easy to find that baby beneath its beam and realize that here was the resplendent miracle of the ages—that this Newborn's cry was the brilliant cry of salvation. For the Light of the World slid into our darkness with a whimper and a need to suck. Nothing regal here.

How astounding to enter that stable and realize that Almighty God had dared to pour all of Himself into dimpled arms and legs to be held in the arms of His creation. Perhaps God knew that if we could recognize and reach out for Him first in this dark unlikely barn, we would go on finding Him in life's dark unlikely days. He still comes to light our darkness.

It started when God said, "Light up the darkness!" and our lives filled up with light as we saw and understood God in the face of Christ, all bright and beautiful.
—2 Corinthians 4:6, The Message

Arise, shine, for your light has come, and the glory of the LORD rises upon you. See, darkness covers the earth and thick darkness is over the peoples, but the LORD rises upon you and his glory appears over you. Nations will come to your light, and kings to the brightness of your dawn.
The sun will no more be your light by day, nor will the brightness of the moon shine on you, for the LORD will be your everlasting light, and your God will be your glory. Your sun will never set again, and your moon will wane no more; the LORD will be your everlasting light, and your days of sorrow will end.
—Isaiah 60:1–3, 19–20

"I, the LORD, have called you in righteousness; I will take hold of your hand. I will keep you and will make you to be a covenant for the people and a light for the Gentiles, to open eyes that are blind, and to free captives from prison and to release from the dungeon those who sit in darkness."

—Isaiah 42:6–7

This is how God showed his love among us: He sent his one and only Son into the world that we might live through him.   —1 John 4:9

Through him all things were made; without him nothing was made that has been made. In him was life, and that life was the light of men. The light shines in the darkness, but the darkness has not understood it.

—John 1:3–5

Who is it that overcomes the world? Only he who believes that Jesus is the Son of God. . . . And this is the testimony; God has given us eternal life, and this life is in his Son. He who has the Son has life, he who does not have the Son of God does not have life.

—1 John 5:5, 11–12

Soaring in His Image

Therefore, if anyone is in Christ, he is a new creation; the old has gone, the new has come!
—2 Corinthians 5:17

Every day I watch hawks sweeping through the canyon outside my window, taking advantage of invisible hills and valleys of wind that allow them to soar. How magnificent they are! How true to their Creator's intention!

As I watch them, I pray, "Father, make me that free and alive. Keep me from scurrying about the underbrush when I could have a place on the lofty currents that pass empty overhead. I waste so much power when I huddle or crawl. I miss seeing so much beauty when I play the role of rodent, burrowing, hiding, and hoarding. You offer me so much—so much mercy for sin, so much grace for living, so much strength for weakness. What is the untested wingspan of Your purpose in me? Oh, Lord, if I do nothing else in my life, may I at least honor You by being, doing, and enjoying what You created me to be, do, and enjoy. Let me soar!"

You were taught, with regard to your former way of life, to put off your old self, which is being corrupted by its deceitful desires; to be made new in the attitude of your minds; and to put on the new self, created to be like God in true righteousness and holiness.

—Ephesians 4:22–24

Do you not know? Have you not heard? The LORD is the everlasting God, the Creator of the ends of the earth. He will not grow tired or weary, and his understanding no one can fathom. He gives strength to the weary and increases the power of the weak. Even youths grow tired and weary, and young men stumble and fall; but those who hope in the LORD will renew their strength. They will soar on wings like eagles; they will run and not grow weary, they will walk and not be faint.

—Isaiah 40:28–31

Going Deeper

He said, "Put out into deep water and let down the nets for a catch."
—Jesus Christ, Luke 5:4

Lord,
It's beginning to seem crowded here
in the shallows where I've always
joyfully splashed in the
waters of salvation,
cooling myself with Your promises,
sipping the waters of grace
from Your hand—
quenching my light thirst.
My thirst is greater now
and yearning toward the deep.
But how I fear
going in over my head!

People drown out there—
die to self—
totally immersed in the mighty
flood of Your righteousness.
Have You made me
dissatisfied, Lord?
Are you,
drawing me
into Your holy depths?
Help me move toward You
in childlike trust, oh
Deep and Living Water!

As the deer pants for streams of water, so my soul pants
for you, O God. My soul thirsts for God, for the living
God. Where can I go and meet with God? Deep calls to
deep in the roar of your waterfalls; all your waves and
breakers have swept over me.
                              —Psalm 42:1–2, 7

You've had a taste of God. Now, like infants at the
breast, drink deep of God's pure kindness. Then you'll
grow up mature and whole in God. . . . As obedient chil-
dren, let yourselves be pulled into a way of life shaped by
God's life, a life energetic and blazing with holiness. God
said, "I am holy; you be holy."
            —1 Peter 2:2; 1:14–16, The Message

"Come, all you who are thirsty, come to the waters . . ."
—Isaiah 55:1

Therefore let us leave the elementary teachings about Christ and go on to maturity.
—Hebrews 6:1

Lord of
the Valleys

I am . . . a lily of the valley.
—Song of Songs 2:1

Very early in life I discovered, much to my delight, that the name *Susan* means "lily." As a representative of such a lovely flower I felt obligated each spring to buy myself a potted lily, watch it bloom, and breathe deeply as it released its sweet scent. This was an enjoyable little private ritual—until a couple of friends educated me as to the true meaning of my name.

While walking with me through my most recent string of trials, testing, and attacks from the enemy, these two friends decided separately to encourage me with one of those small gift cards that tells the meaning of a person's name and cites an appropriate verse of Scripture. The verse and picture on each of the cards was different, but the meaning given for my name was the same. Surprisingly, however, the flower my name comes from is not "Lily" but "Lily of the Valley." Oh my.

Perhaps that helps to explain things of late. I'm not the lily I thought I was. If I had known about the "valley clause" I might have changed my name before it was too late!

This is a lily of an entirely different sort. Fragrant and lovely, yes, but it grows its cascade of tiny bell-like blooms in the lowlands—down in the valleys of life. No mountaintop vistas for this little beauty.

It's easy for those of us who are "valley-dwellers" to feel lost down here in life's shaded ravines— swamped by the rain that so often falls here. At times we feel hidden from God's attention, care, and help, especially when we're being pelted by torrential downpours. But when our Lord declared, "I am with you always" (Matthew 28:20), His promise included those of us planted in the bottomlands, depressions, and gullies of life. He is here to help us grow strong in the face of all that comes to us, for He declares Himself to be not only the God of the mountaintops, but also the God of the valleys.

As proof of this, He led me to a remarkable passage in 1 Kings 20, which tells the story of Israel being threatened by the vast Aramean forces in the hills outside Samaria. We who are weak and besieged are encouraged to realize how God enabled the relatively small armies of Ahab, king of Israel, to defeat the vast Aramean armies led by King Aram and the thirty-two kings allied with him.

Then, even though God had given Israel the victory in this battle, He continued to take thoughtful care of His people by warning them to fortify for another attack from the Arameans the following spring (vv. 13–22).

Meanwhile, the Arameans thought they knew why they had been overpowered. They had fought in the hills, and they figured that Israel's high and holy "god of the hills" could easily protect them in such places! So they decided to wage war on the plains where "surely we will be stronger than they" (v. 25).

So in the spring the Arameans confidently covered the countryside with their troops, looking scornfully across at the Israelites camped opposite them "like two small flocks of goats" (v. 27). It must have been quite a scene. But God had another surprise for them.

As God's people stood in the valley, probably overwhelmed by the odds facing them, God said to them: "Because the Arameans think the Lord is a god of the hills and not a god of the valleys, I will deliver this vast army into your hands, and you will know that I am the Lord" (v. 28).

Thank you, mighty Lord of the Valleys. It's not so bad being a lily of the valley with You here to protect me.

Even though I walk through the valley of the shadow of death, I will fear no evil, for you are with me, your rod and your staff, they comfort me. You prepare a table before me in the presence of my enemies.
—Psalm 23:4–5

"So do not fear, for I am with you; do not be dismayed, for I am your God. I will strengthen you and help you; I will uphold you with my righteous right hand. All who rage against you will surely be ashamed and disgraced; those who oppose you will be as nothing and perish. Though you search for your enemies, you will not find them. Those who wage war against you will be nothing at all. For I am the Lord, your God, who takes hold of your right hand and says to you, Do not fear; I will help you.
"I will make . . . springs within the valleys."
—Isaiah 41:10–13, 18

Safe on Top of Everything

Whoever trusts in the LORD is kept safe.
—Proverbs 29:25

When wicked men would not repent,
God's rain of judgment soon was sent.
So God said, "Noah build a boat,
an ark of promise that will float
above the flood and let you sing,
safe on top of everything."

When heartaches rain from heavy skies,
and troubled waters round me rise,
then I will build a place to hide.
Upon God's promise I will ride
on storm-tossed seas until I sing,
safe on top of everything.

As evil reigned in Noah's day
it will again, but we won't stay!
God promised that if we abide
in the Ark of Christ, one day we'll rise
above this world and forever sing,
safe on top of everything!*

"Oh, that I had the wings of a dove! I would fly away and
be at rest. . . . I would hurry to my place of shelter, far
from the tempest and storm."
                                        —Psalm 55: 6, 8

For in the day of trouble he will keep me safe in his dwelling; he will hide me in the shelter of his tabernacle and set
me high upon a rock.   —Psalm 27:5

If you fully obey the LORD your God and carefully follow
all his commands I give you today, the LORD your God
will set you high above all the nations on earth. . . you
will always be at the top, never at the bottom.
                                        —Deuteronomy 28:1, 13

O LORD, you are my God; I will exalt you and praise
your name, for in perfect faithfulness you have done
marvelous things, things planned long ago. . . You have
been a refuge for the poor, a refuge for the needy in his
distress, a shelter from the storm.
                                        —Isaiah 25:1, 4

* Special thanks to Mary A. Myers for permitting me to use
the lovely progression of thought from her poem (of the same
title), rewriting it into a song. The verses to that song appear

here. Mary is a precious eighty-six-year-old sister in Christ who has "adopted me" across a continent, delighting me with her fertile mind and showering me with her prayers, love, and encouragement.

An Umbrella
of Love

You have been . . . a refuge for the needy in his distress, a shelter from the storm.
—Isaiah 25:4

There is one gain that comes only to those who are caught out in the rain, and it comes through God's dear family. It is the blessing of finding oneself in the midst of one of life's raging storms and yet be sheltered under the faithful care of God's people—covered over by intercessory prayer—protected by practical acts of love. My family and I are standing, right now, beneath just such an umbrella of love, and it is precious beyond description.

I would not have signed up for this blessing, yet I would not trade for anything on earth this sense of being enfolded in God's vast family. All around the world people are praying for my husband, Herb, in his battle with cancer. Letters, cards, calls, and notes of encouragement have come daily with promises of prayer and reminders of God's faithfulness in spite of the steady progression of this terrible disease.

Sometimes I picture God being pelted with prayers and pleas on my husband's behalf.

Then my dear encourager, Mary Myers, wrote from Florida, painting a slightly different scene. She had been "visiting us" via one of her creative prayer-times and wrote, "A little bit ago I dropped in your place with a few promises for Herb, and he was one sight to behold!"

And this is what she saw, in spite of the fact that she has been physically blinded by macular degeneration: "He was lying on, wrapped up in, festooned with, covered over with thousands and thousands of prayers and promises, promises and prayers; and the glory and fragrance filled your home and hearts."

And I breathed, recalling the "golden bowls full of incense, which are the prayers of the saints" (Revelation 5:8).

"So," Mary went on, "I left my greeting atop all the others—and the sight of Herb so festooned set me to quietly laughing inside, and I haven't quit yet."

And the picture of frail, white-haired Mary lying alone in bed (quite ill herself) laughing in the joy of the Lord and in the loving prayers of God's great family, set me to smiling and rejoicing inside. And I found that I, too, wanted to decorate others just as beautifully.

So I sent out prayers and promises, promises and prayers, to cover Mary and all of you, my dear brothers and sisters in Christ, who have prayed in loving faith seeking God's very best for us as we trust Him day by day.

And this is my prayer: that your love may abound more and more in knowledge and depth of insight, so that you may be able to discern what is best and may be pure and blameless until the day of Christ, filled with the fruit of righteousness that comes through Jesus Christ—to the glory and praise of God.
—Philippians 1:9–11

For this reason I kneel before the Father, from whom his whole family in heaven and earth derives its name. I pray that out of his glorious riches he may strengthen you with power through his Spirit in your inner being, so that Christ may dwell in your hearts through faith. And I pray that you, being rooted and established in love, may have power, together with all the saints, to grasp how wide and long and high and deep is the love of Christ, and to know this love that surpasses knowledge—that you may be filled to the measure of all the fullness of God.
—Ephesians 3:14–19

I'm Growing!

But grow in the grace and knowledge of our Lord and Savior, Jesus Christ. To him be glory both now and forever! Amen.

—2 Peter 3:18

I keep reaching for You,
God,
and over and over I
find that
You reached first,
and so much
farther.
I keep reaching for You
Lord,
and over and over I
find that
I touch others

on my way to You.
I keep reaching for You,
Jesus,
and over and over I
find that
my arms are stretching.
I'm growing.

I'm off and running, and I'm not turning back.

So let's keep focused on that goal, those of us who want everything God has for us. If any of you have something else in mind, something less than total commitment, God will clear your blurred vision—you'll see it yet! Now that we're on the right track, let's stay on it.

Stick with me, friends. . . .

We're waiting the arrival of the Savior, the Master, Jesus Christ, who will transform our earthly bodies into glorious bodies like his own. He'll make us beautiful and whole with the same powerful skill by which he is putting everything as it should be, under and around him.

My dear, dear friends! I love you so much. I do want the very best for you. You make me feel such joy, fill me with such pride. Don't waver. Stay on track, steady in God.

—Philippians 3:14–4:1, The Message

Note to the Reader

The publisher invites you to share your response to the message of this book by writing Discovery House Publishers, Box 3566, Grand Rapids, MI 49501, USA. For information about other Discovery House books, music, or videos, contact us at the same address or call 1-800-653-8333. Find us on the Internet at http://www.dhp.org/ or send e-mail to books@dhp.org.